"And into the forest I go, to lose my mind and find my soul."

— John Muir

Road Tripping
AMERICA'S
National Parks

DISCLAIMER: The following information is to be used at your own risk. The included maps are for trip planning purposes only and are not suitable for navigation. Obtain USGS Topographic Maps for trail navigation. Check current park regulations before you embark on this journey. No liability is assumed for losses or damages due to the information provided. The author is not a medical professional. Consult a doctor if you are concerned about health risks. You are responsible for your own choices, actions, and results.

ISBN: 978-0-9851772-3-2
Library of Congress Control Number: 2025910498

Published by Open Media Arts June 1 2025   www.openmediaarts.com

TABLE OF CONTENTS

Gear List

Kitchen Shelter
Canopy
Stakes & Guy-lines
Towels / Bucket

Sleep Shelter
Tent
Footprint
Stakes & Guy-lines

Furniture
Chairs
Table
Mattress
Fan

Bedding
Sheets
Blankets
Comforter
Pillows

Food Storage
Cooler / Fridge
Ice Packs
Battery
Cables

Food Preparation
Stove
Fuel
Electric Kettle

Cookware
Pots
Pans
Utensils
Coffee Maker

Toiletries
Toilet Paper
Toothbrush
Toothpaste
Soap

Day Pack
Hip pack
Backpack
Stuff Sacks

Ten Essentials
First Aid / Knife / Sunscreen
Compass & Map / Fire
Headlamp / Food / Water
Shelter / Clothing

Nutrition
Food
Water
Electrolytes

Gear Storage
Bins
Bags
Containers

Underwear
Bottoms
Tops
Socks

Base Layer
Long Bottoms
Long Tops

Mid Layer
Shorts
Long Shirt & Pants
Fleece

Outer Layer
Down Jacket
Rain Jacket

Head
Cap
Wool Hat
Sunglasses
Sunscreen

LOCATION	DISTANCE	TIME
Albany, NY	0 mi	0:00
Thatcher State Park, NY	22 mi	0:30
Buttermilk Falls State Park, NY	174 mi	3:20
Watkins Glen State Park, NY	200 mi	4:15
Total	200 mi	4:15

Campground

Six Nations Campground
3530 State Route 419, Watkins Glen NY 14891
(607)535-4511
42.36861,-76.90111

Mouse

1

Day 1 *Activities*

HIKE: Indian Ladder
1 mi 328' elv 0:45 MODERATE

Features of this trail include a sheer limestone cliff wall, an arching cave, several streams, and a waterfall that the trail goes beneath.

A trail with many steps descends to the base of the falls. At the end of the trail there is a steep climb up to the trail exit above the escarpment.

Location
830 Thacher Park Road
Voorheesville, NY 12186
(518) 872-1237
42.654645, -74.017630

HIKE: Buttermilk Falls
1.6 mi 462' elv 1:00 MODERATE

This heavily shaded trail follows a rapidly dropping gorge past several cascades and a total of ten waterfalls. The main Buttermilk Falls is 165' high, divided into two sections, with a large swimmable pool at its base. Stone pillars and creek bed potholes add to the character of the glen as the trail climbs beside it on many stone stairs. Pulpit rock and falls is a 42' high formation towards the top of the gorge. From Pulpit falls one can return the way they came on the gorge trail or form a loop via the rim trail.

Location
106 E. Buttermilk Falls Rd. (Off Rt. 13 S)
Ithaca, NY 14850
(607) 273-5761
42.41761, -76.52318

Tips: Food Storage & Disposal

As this trip progresses you will be entering areas where wildlife is the only permanent resident. When visiting their homes it is essential that you follow the rules of the park. Ask a ranger and they will provide you with each parks regulations.

Yellowstone, Glacier, Mount Rainier, Olympic and Lassen have the following rules:

In front-country areas (e.g. campgrounds and trailheads) food and other attractants such as toiletries and first aid items should be locked in vehicles with the windows and doors closed or In bear-proof food storage boxes provided at many front-country campsites. Food should only be out of storage when in sight. After cooking all utensils should be cleaned and stored back in a closed vehicle or bear proof container. Cleaning should be done where you cook in a bucket that is then brought to a disposal facility and strained so that food particles can be disposed of as trash and the grey water can be either flushed down a toilet or poured into a waste water facility. All food scraps and packaging should be disposed of in a bear proof dumpster or trash can. Do not cook where you sleep. Set up your tent as far as possible from where you cook and eat. Yosemite does not permit food being stored in a vehicle and requires the use of provided bear boxes.

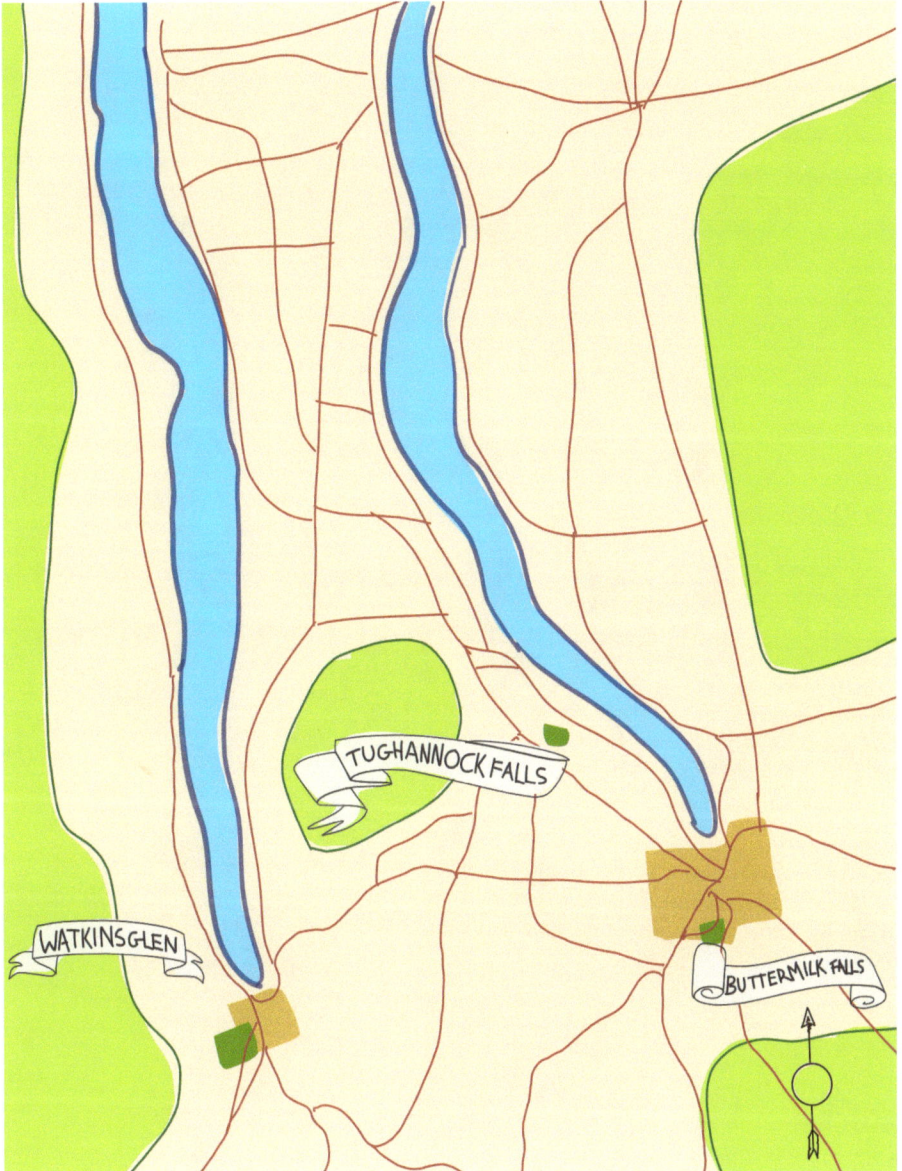

Campground

Six Nations Campground
3530 State Route 419, Watkins Glen NY 14891
(607)535-4511
42.36861,-76.90111

Watkins Glen

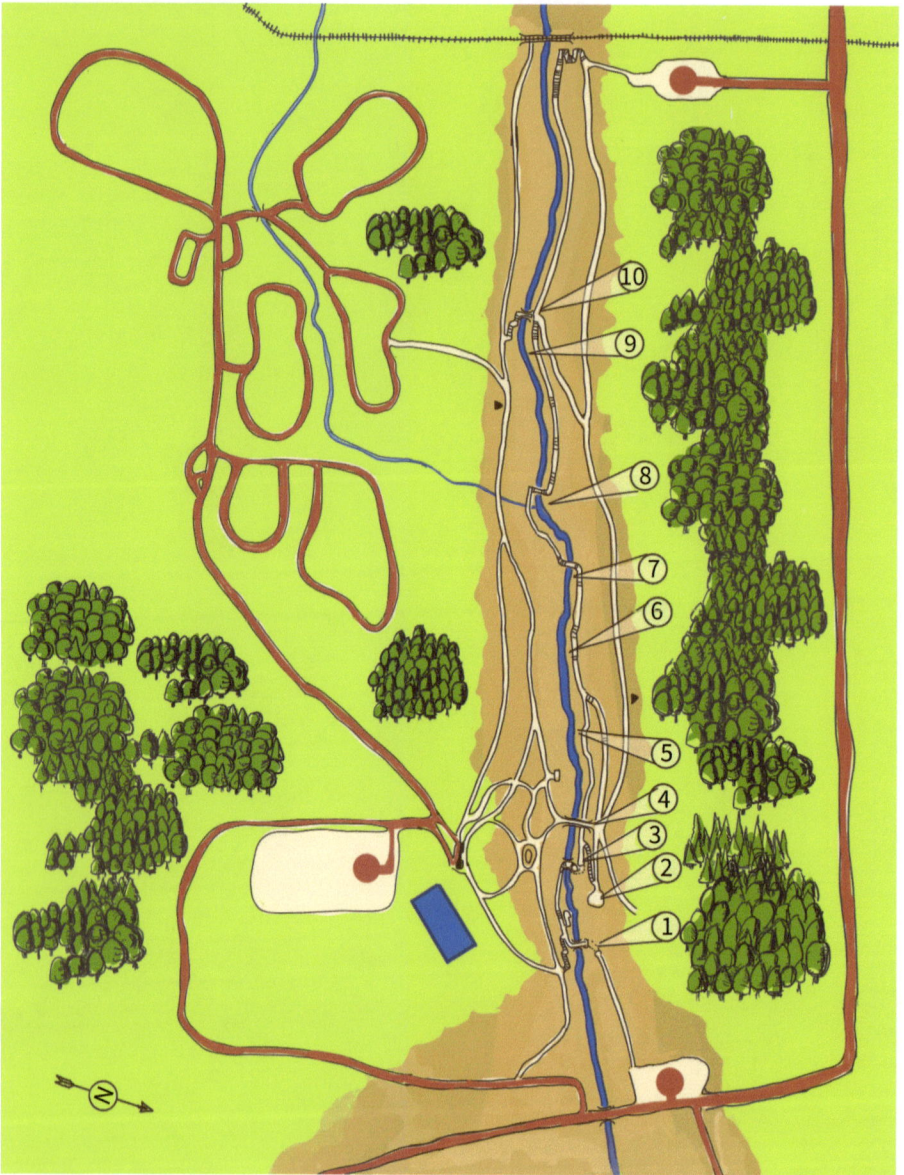

FEATURE

1. Entrance Tunnel
2. Cavern Cascade
3. Point Lookout
4. Spiral Tunnel
5. The Narrows

6. Glen Cathedral
7. Central Cascade
8. Rainbow Falls
9. Spiral Gorge
10. Mile Point Bridge

Day 2 *Activities*

HIKE: Watkins Glen
3.0 mi 500' elv 2:00 EASY

Following a stunning sheer rock wall gorge this trail climbs 800 stone steps as it passes 19 waterfalls.

From the campground entrance a figure eight loop can be made by crossing mile point bridge and climbing out of the gorge to the upper entrance then descending Jacobs ladder back into the gorge. Follow the gorge down past many cascades passing mile point bridge below frowning cliff to rainbow falls. Continue in the gorge past Central Cascade and Glen Cathedral. Pass the suspension bridge. Cross the creek at Cavern Cascade and before crossing back again at the Sentry Bridge ascend Couch's Staircase. Follow this uphill trail to the Lily Pond and back down to cross the suspension bridge. Go uphill to the Lovers Lane Lookout staying above Frowning Cliff and descending to Mile Point Bridge and back to the campground the way you came in.

Location
Starts at campground.

HIKE: Deckertown Falls
.3 mi 50' elv 0:30 EASY

Deckertown Falls, is a lesser-known, but fascinating series of cascades in the town of Montour that has a large swimmable pool at its base.

Deckertown Falls is a series of three drops that are easily seen from a small path that leads from the parking area to the creek. The falls starts out as a 30ft long cascade into a shallow pool on a ledge, which then drops a few feet down a small wide cascade not visible from the main vantage point and then finally down a fast-moving chute and into a very deep pool.

Upstream, heading towards the Rt 224 bridge are a few more cascades that can't be seen without scrambling up the muddy trail to the right of Deckertown Falls.

Location
42.3434152, -76.8309777

HIKE: Taughannock Falls Gorge Trail
1.8 mi 242' elv 0:45 EASY

A scenic and popular waterfall

The Gorge Trail follows Taughannock Creek for one mile before reaching the tallest single-drop waterfall east of the Rocky Mountains. At 215' Taughannock Falls is a sight to behold. One more waterfall can be viewed from the Gorge Trail, known as Little or Lower Falls. It is located just steps from the lower trailhead.

Location
42.545671, -76.59948

Tips: The Ten Essentials

When traveling into the great outdoors you may not just be going for a walk in the park. In order to ensure a safe adventure it is recommended that you always bring the ten essentials.

1 Navigation: map, compass, altimeter, GPS device

2 Sun protection: sunglasses, hat and sunscreen

3 Extra clothes beyond the minimum expectation

4 Flashlight and extra batteries

5 First aid including foot care and insect repellent

6 Fire, matches, lighter, tinder

7 Knife

8 Extra food beyond the minimum expectation

9 Extra water and purifier

10 Emergency shelter (a small tarp)

Navigation   Sun Protection   Extra Layers

Flashlight   First Aid   Fire

Knife   Food   Water

Shelter

Navigation
Never trust in a smartphone as your only navigational aid. GPS devices can be loaded with route information for each trip and function as altimeter and compass which can be used in conjunction with a proper topographical map to find your location.

Sun Protection
When above tree line or in the desert the body and eyes become prone to burning.

Extra Clothing
Always bring a rain jacket, lightweight long underwear top and bottom, and a hat.

First Aid
Blister care and other bandages, kinesiology tape for strains and sprains, antihistamine and anti inflammatory medications, tweezers for ticks and splinters.

Water
A small water filter is essential and carry some chemical purification just in case.

Emergency Shelter
A small ultralight tarp and a rapid pitch ridge-line can be as small as a can of soda.

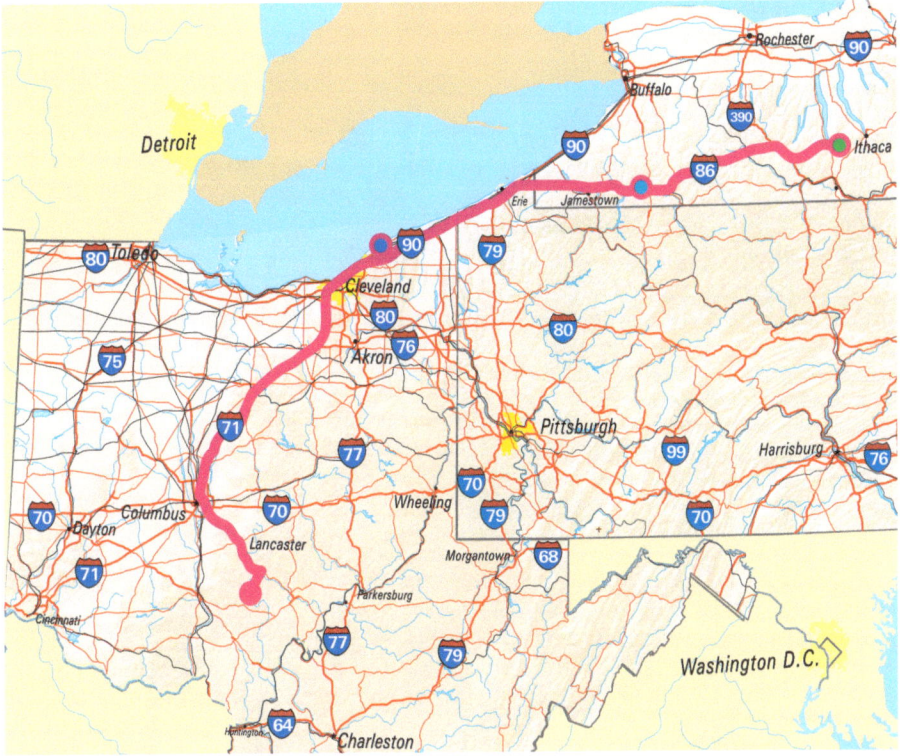

LOCATION	DISTANCE	TIME
Watkins Glen State Park, NY	0 mi	0:00
Allegany State Park, NY	129 mi	2:00
Headlands Beach State Park, OH	281 mi	4:20
Hocking Hills, OH	508 mi	7:50
Total	508 mi	7:50

Campground

Hocking Hills State Park Campground
19852 ST. RT 664 S Logan, OH 43138
(740)385-6842
39.43372, -82.54824

Gopher

Day 3 *Activities*

VIEW: Stone Tower

The stone tower was completed in 1934 by the civilian conservation corps and provides views of Salamanca to the north and Red House Lake to the south.

Location
2373 ASP, Rte 1, Suite 3
Salamanca, NY 14779
(716) 379-6450
42.10286, -78.74452

RELAX: Headlands Beach

This half mile long natural sand beach along Lake Erie offers swimming and walking.

Location
9601 Headlands Road
Mentor, OH 44060
(440) 466-8400
41.7573, -81.2892

Tips: Navigation

As this trip progresses the hikes will become longer and route finding will become more difficult. ALWAYS CARRY A USGS TOPOGRAPHIC MAP. The use of a compass and altimeter are analog methods of locating oneself on a map and determining the proper directions to follow. GPS devices can be operated in a similar fashion and have the advantage of being programmed with routes that are loaded into the device and give directions as you hike. Some devices even have topographic data. I prefer to use a GPS watch that does not have topographic data but has excellent battery life. Smartphones run out of battery too quickly in my opinion, but if that's your preferred method bring an extra battery bank. Satellite Communicators are also useful and allow you to check in with someone or function as an emergency beacon for Search and Rescue.

Always leave a plan with someone you are not traveling with and a check in time so that if you don't make it out someone knows where you were planning to go.

Tips: Wilderness Leadership

Many of this authors outdoor skills where learned by attending a 50 day Colorado Outward Bound Wilderness Leadership Program. NOLS is another organization with similar courses, and now many universities are offering programs as search and rescue has become a more defined career path.

Be prepared at all times with the Ten Essentials. Learn proper navigation skills. Be prepared to perform emergency first aid.

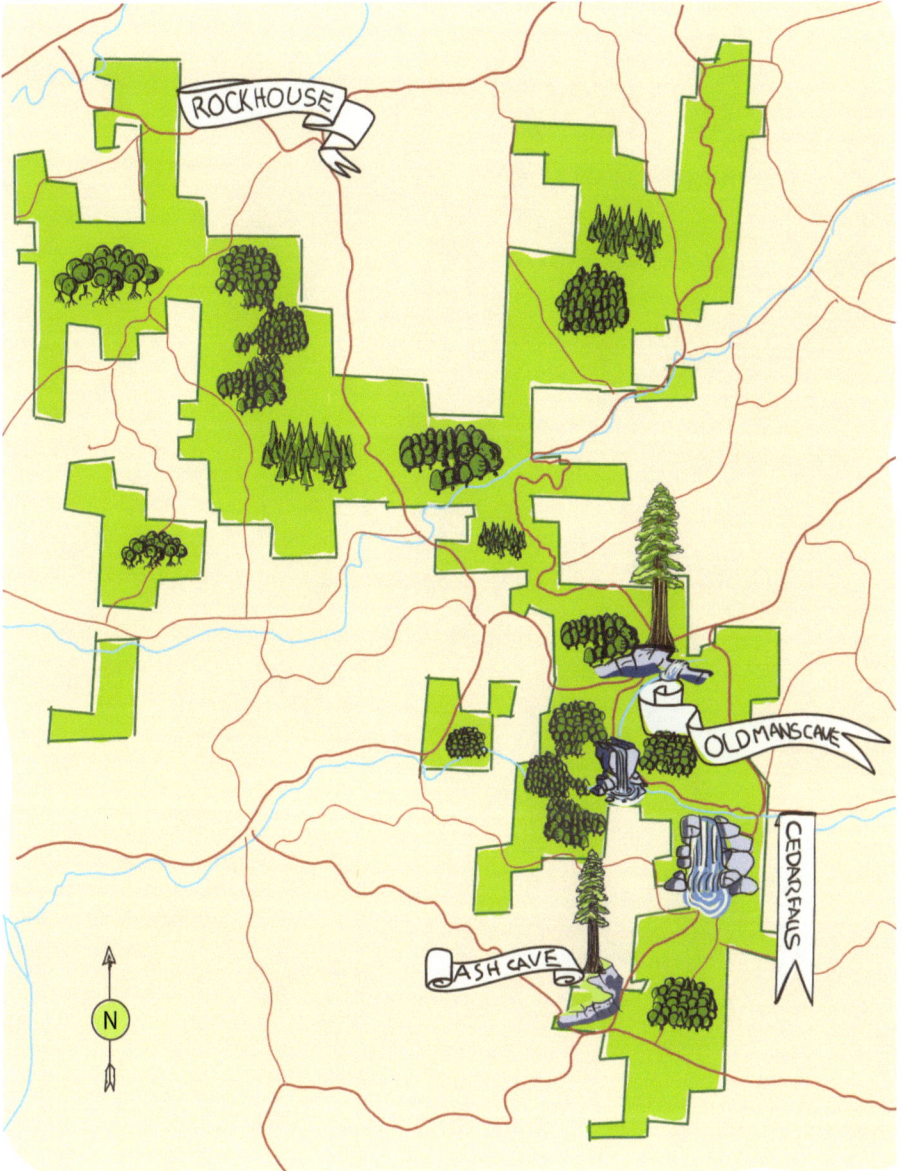

Campground

Hocking Hills State Park Campground
19852 ST. RT 664 S Logan, OH 43138
(740)385-6842
39.43372, -82.54824

Old Man's Cave

FEATURE

1. Upper Falls
2. Devils Bathtub
3. Whale in the Wall
4. Eagle Rock
5. A-Frame Bridge
6. Old Man's Cave
7. Sphinx Head
8. Lower Falls
9. Broken Rock Falls

Day 4 *Activities*

HIKE: Old Man's Cave
2 mi 150' elv 1:30 EASY

This hike includes deep tree shaded valleys, multiple waterfalls and a cave that was once inhabited by a hermit.

From the campground head towards the A Frame Bridge on the northern most trail. Before the bridge turn right on the Gorge Overlook Trail. Upon reaching the park road take a left and walk the road a short distance to the upper entrance of the Buckeye Trail. Follow the Buckeye Trail to the top of the Upper Falls. This is the start of the Upper Falls Loop Trail. Descend the staircase on Grandma Gatewood (Buckeye) trail to the bottom of the Upper Falls. Follow this trail down the gorge to a bridge over Devil's Bathtub. After going through a small tunnel you will arrive at a spur trail to Old Man's Cave. Back on the main trail, the next feature you will pass is the Sphinx head before descending to the Lower Falls.

HIKE: Cedar Falls
2 mi 100' elv 1:30 EASY

Cedar Falls is in a chasm bound by hemlock trees that features a tranquil grotto at the waterfalls base.

From the campground take the Rose Lake Trail along the east shore to the intersection with the Gorge Overlook Trail at the southern end of the lake.From here follow the Overlook Trail to the bottom of Cedar Falls.

Location
Starts at campground.

Tips: Hypothermia

Hypothermia is a serious threat in the outdoors. What starts out as a warm day can quickly turn into a windy, wet, and cold outing. The best defense is to keep moving, but if an injury or other obstacle keeps you from doing so, your body temperature will drop in a matter of minutes. When stopping put on extra layers. A warm hat, a down vest, and a rain jacket are always in my kit. Always carry the ten essentials.

How to Treat Hypothermia

Take the person's temperature. If it is below 95 degrees the situation is an emergency. Try to find shelter. Remove any wet clothing from the victim. Warm the center of the body first. Use skin-to-skin contact under loose, dry layers of blankets, clothing, towels, or sheets. Provide the victim with warm beverages. Keep the person dry and wrapped. Stay with the person until medical help arrives.

Tips: 7 Principles of Leave No Trace

1   Plan Ahead and Prepare

2   Travel and Camp on
     Durable Surfaces

3   Dispose of Waste Properly

4   Leave What You Find

5   Minimize Campfire Impacts

6   Respect Wildlife

7   Be Considered of Others

Plan
Ahead

Travel & Camp on
Durable Surfaces

Dispose of
Waste Properly

Leave
What You
Find

Fire
Responsibility

Respect
Wildlife

Respect
Others

Plan Ahead and Prepare
Know the regulations for the areas you'll visit. Prepare for extreme weather, hazards, and emergencies. Repackage food to minimize waste and pack a trash bag. Use a map and compass or GPS with trail routes prepared in advance.

Travel and Camp on Durable Surfaces
Durable surfaces include maintained trails and designated campsites, rock, gravel, sand, dry grasses or snow. Walk single file in the middle of the trail, even when wet or muddy. In areas without trails try not to use the same route that others have used and do not go off trail if prohibited.

Dispose of Waste Properly
Pack it in, pack it out. Utilize toilet facilities whenever possible. Otherwise, deposit solid human waste in cat holes dug 6 to 8 inches deep, at least 200 feet from water, camp and trails. Cover and disguise the cat hole when finished. To wash yourself or your dishes, carry water 200 feet away from streams or lakes and use small amounts of biodegradable soap. Scatter strained dishwater.

Leave What You Find
Take only memories and leave only footprints (try not to leave footprints if possible).

Minimize Campfire Impacts
Where permitted, use established fire rings. Burn all wood to coals and smother out.

Respect Wildlife
Observe wildlife from a distance. Do not follow or approach them.

Be Considerate of Others
Be courteous. Yield to other users on the trail. Let nature's sounds prevail. Avoid loud voices and noises. Take breaks and camp away from trails and other visitors.

Day 5
Hocking Hills, OH - Coon Creek, IL

	LOCATION	DISTANCE	TIME
🟢	Hocking Hills, OH	0 mi	0
🔵	Springwood Park, IN	166 mi	2:30
🔵	Fern Cliff Nature Preserve, IN	291 mi	4:30
🔴	Coon Creek Campground, IL	408 mi	6:45
	Total	408 mi	6:45

Campground

Coon Creek Campground
1989 State Hwy 16, Shelbyville, IL 62565
(217) 774-3951
39.4513889, -88.7625

Loon

13

Day 5 *Activities*

RELAX: Springwood Park, IN

Across the street from Springwood park is a short trail (Whitewater Gorge Park trail) to Thistlethwaite Falls.

Location
Springwood Park
Waterfall Rd, Richmond, IN 47374
39.851849, -84.899743

HIKE: Fern Cliff Nature Preserve, IN
1.2 mi 157' elv :30 EASY

A short trail leads to fern covered sandstone cliffs.

Location
37.5429567, -88.9798353

DISCLAIMER: In a couple of days this trip enters Grizzly Bear territory. The following information is to be used at your own risk. Always check with each park for current policies. Bear spray is not permitted in Yosemite National Park since they have a non aggressive to human bear population. Always follow proper food storage as recommended by each park.

When in Bear Country
Travel in groups and keep up the conversation

BE
BEAR
AWARE

If You See a Bear
Announce yourself in a calm voice. DO NOT RUN!

Black Bear
Black Color
Big Butt & Ears

Phase 1: Encounter
Slowly back away

Phase 2: Bear Approaches
Raise arms and make noise

Phase 3: Attack
Fight back

Grizzly Bear
Brown Color
Big Shoulders

Phase 1: Encounter
Slowly back away

Phase 2: Bear Approaches
Deploy bear spray at 30 feet

Phase 3: Attack
Play dead, cover neck

Day 6

Coon Creek, IL - Sioux Falls, SD

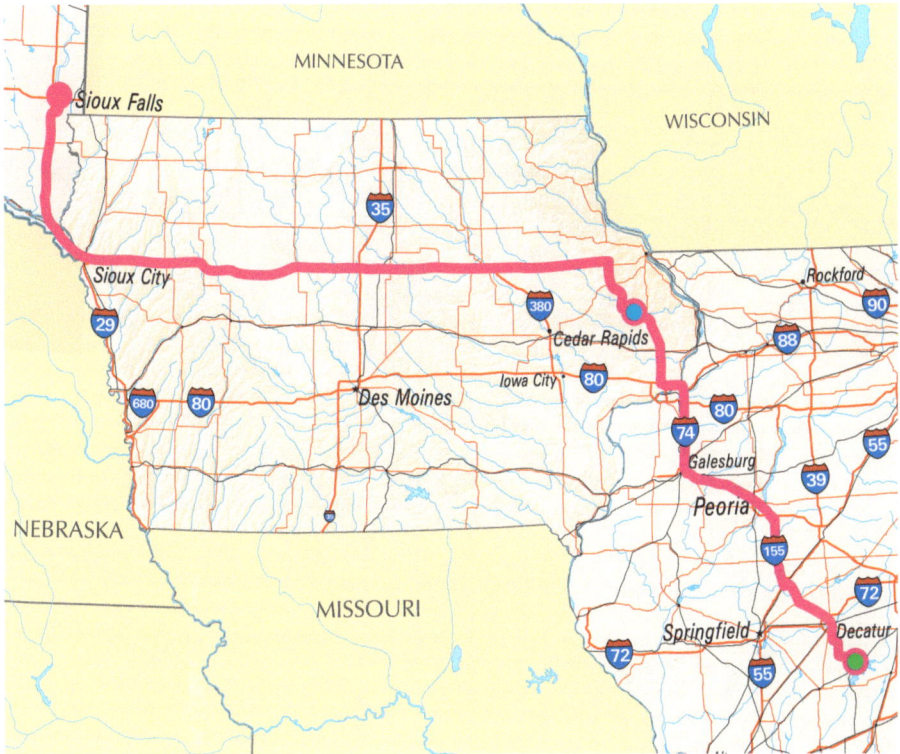

LOCATION	DISTANCE	TIME
🟢 Coon Creek Campground, IL	0 mi	0:00
🔵 Maquoketa Caves, IA	261 mi	4:00
🔴 Sioux Falls, SD	668 mi	10:00
Total	668 mi	10:00

Lodging

Towneplace Suites Sioux Falls
4545 W Homefield Dr, Sioux Falls, SD, 57106
(605) 361-2626
43.52848, -96.78345

Day 6 *Activities*

HIKE: Maquoketa Caves, IA
1.7 mi 288' elv 0:50 EASY

The trail system here is broken into many segments named for their primary destination however these short spurs can be joined into a figure eight loop that visits over a dozen caves.

Dancehall cave is the largest feature in the park and is approximately 800' long with three entrances. Dancehall cave is tall enough that one can walk upright almost the entire length of the cave. After visiting Dancehall, hike along the western loop to visit Rainy Day, Ice, and Barbell caves.

Location
9688 Caves Rd Maquoketa, IA 52060
42.12363, -90.76576

RESUPPLY: ALDI Sioux Falls
2808 S Louise Ave, Sioux Falls, SD 57106
43.5199900, -96.7709124

Tips: Bear Spray

**BE
BEAR
AWARE**

Keep bear spray in a holster within easy reach.
Bears may false charge then stop. Stay calm.
Follow bear aware protocols.
Wait until bear is within 30' before spraying.

Step 1

Place forefinger through hole in handle with thumb on safety clip curl. Pull safety clip straight back and off using thumb.

Step 2

Depress actuator tab for burst of spray.
Aim at face and eyes of bear.
Press trigger for 2 seconds to create a barrier of spray between you and the bear.
Stop to evaluate the impact of wind and adjust your aim if needed before spraying again.

Step 3

Replace safety clip by firmly pushing with thumb until audible "snap" is heard. Check to see if safety clip is securely in place. No gap should be visible between the actuator handle and the safety clip.

DO NOT KEEP BEAR SPRAY IN A HOT CAR WITHOUT A PROPER TRAVEL CONTAINER.
IT MAY EXPLODE.

Day 7

Sioux Falls, SD - Custer State Park, SD

	LOCATION	DISTANCE	TIME
🟢	Sioux Falls, SD	0 mi	0:00
🔵	Ben Reifel Visitors Center, SD	280 mi	4:00
🔵	The Notch Trail, SD	282 mi	4:05
🔵	Bigfoot Pass Overlook, SD	288 mi	4:15
🟡	Pinnacles Overlook, SD	302 mi	4:40
🟠	Mount Rushmore, SD	408 mi	6:40
🔴	Sylvan Lake Campground, SD	422 mi	7:15
	Total	422 mi	7:15

Campground

Custer State Park Sylvan Lake Campground
13329 US Highway 16A, Custer, SD 57730
(605) 394-2693
43.83925, -103.55605

Wild Donkey

Day 7 *Activities*

LEARN: Reifel Visitors Center

The Ben Reifel Visitors Center center features a fossil preparation lab and exhibits.

Location
25216 Ben Reifel Road Interior, SD 57750
43.74898, -101.94174

HIKE: The Notch Trail
1.2 mi 270' elv 0:30 EASY

A short but fun way to explore the Badlands of South Dakota. This is located before the visitors center but has no facilities so a short backtrack is in order.

The hike starts winding its way into the bluffs before ascending a challenging hanging ladder to reach the ridge.

Location
43.7565625, -101.9294375

VIEW: Bigfoot Pass Overlook

A short boardwalk leads to this overlook of the Badlands.

Location
43.7951221, -102.0446111

VIEW: Pinnacles Overlook

This is the most expansive overlook in this section of the badlands.

Location
43.8698234, -102.2329208

DRIVE: Iron Mountain Road

The Iron Mountain Road is 17 miles long with 314 curves, 14 switchbacks, 3 pigtails, and 3 tunnels. Senator Norbeck was the visionary behind the roads construction along with architect C. C. Gideon who mapped the winding route to Mount Rushmore.

Location
43.77282, -103.33945

HIKE: Mount Rushmore

The Presidents Trail provides different views of the monument featuring the famous four presidents: George Washington, Thomas Jefferson, Theodore Rosevelt, and Abraham Lincoln.

Location
43.8789472, -103.459825

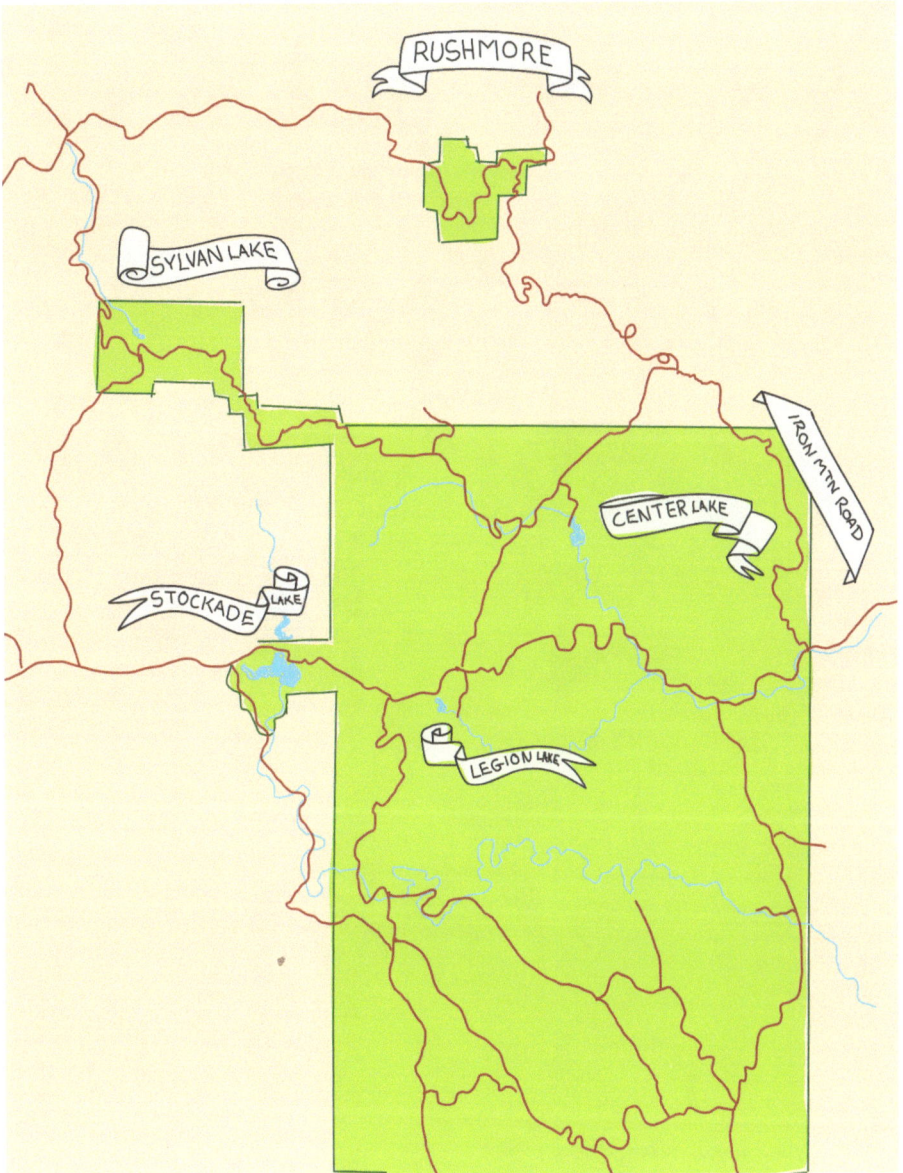

Campground

Custer State Park Sylvan Lake Campground
13329 US Highway 16A, Custer, SD 57730
(605) 394-2693
43.83925, -103.55605

Sylvan Lake - Sunday Gulch

FEATURE

1. Campground Connector
2. Sylvan Lake Beach
3. Gradual Elevation Sunday Gulch
4. Rapid Elevation Sunday Gulch
5. Creek Crossing

Day 8 *Activities*

HIKE: Sylvan Lake - Sunday Gulch Loop
5.5 mi 805' elv 2:30 MODERATE

This hike features both the easy stroll around Sylvan Lake and the gullies and rock scrambles of Sunday Gulch.

From the campground follow the connector trail .5 miles to the lake. Follow the Sylvan Lake Shore Trail to the far end of the lake. Hiking the Sunday Gulch Loop clockwise starts by entering a crack in the rocks and climbs steadily through the rock spires. After the trail levels out it meanders through open forest with views of the surrounding mountains. After crossing a few small streams and waterfall you enter a cool, rocky glen with many water features. From here there are a series of steps and handrails that wind around the boulders of the gulch bringing you quickly up in elevation back to Sylvan Lake.

Location
Starts at campground.

History: Black Hills

The Black Hills were a sacred territory for several Native American tribes, particularly the Lakota Sioux, who called it "Paha Sapa" - The center of the universe.

After conquering the Cheyenne in 1776, the Lakota took the territory of the Black Hills as their own. They would control the area for almost one hundred years. In 1868, the federal US government signed the Fort Laramie Treaty, establishing the Great Sioux Reservation west of the Missouri River. This treaty exempted the Black Hills from all non-indigenous settlement "forever". However, when gold was discovered as a result of George Armstrong Custer's Black Hills Expedition of 1874, a gold rush swept the area and conflicts arose as settlers wanted what had been given to the Lakota. The US government conquered the Black Hills by military force and relocated the Lakota to five smaller reservations in western South Dakota.

The location of what is now Mount Rushmore was a sacred site to the Lakota. It was called The Six Grandfathers (Tȟuŋkášila Šákpe) and got its name from Lakota medicine man Nicholas Black Elk after receiving a vision.

"The vision was of the six sacred directions: west, east, north, south, above, and below. The directions were said to represent kindness and love, full of years and wisdom, like human grandfathers." - *Nicholas Black Elk*

History: Mount Rushmore

In 1923 South Dakota State Historian Doane Robinson suggested a sculpture in the Black Hills that would draw tourists to the area. Originally the idea was to depict the mountain men and Indians that had become folk legends of the area. While trying to acquire funding for the sculptures it was determined that making it a monument to the United States Presidents would have greater appeal to those who might provide financial backing.

In 1925 the location was chosen and dedicated as a National Monument site. In 1927 President Coolidge handed the sculptor Gutzon Borglum a set of drill bits, and sculpting began. In 1930 Washington was dedicated. In 1936 Jefferson was dedicated. In 1937 Lincoln was dedicated. In 1939 Rosevelt was dedicated. Gutzon Borglum died in 1941 and his son Lincoln Borglum took over the completion of the monument.

George Washington, 1732-1799

The First President of the United States who led the revolution establishing independence from the British Empire.

Thomas Jefferson, 1742-1826

The Third President of the United States was the primary author of the Declaration of Independence.

Theodore Rosevelt, 1858-1919

The 26th President of the United States was instrumental in negotiating the construction of the Panama Canal, linking the Atlantic and the Pacific.

Abraham Lincoln, 1809-1865

The 16th President of the United States is known for holding the country together during the Civil War and abolishing slavery.

Custer State Park, SD - Yellowstone National Park, WY

LOCATION		DISTANCE	TIME
🟢	Sylvan Lake Campground, SD	0 mi	0:00
🔵	Devils Tower, WY	118 mi	2:15
🔵	Shell Falls, WY	352 mi	6:10
🔴	Canyon Campground, WY	525 mi	9:40
	Total	525 mi	9:40

Campground

Canyon Campground
Yellowstone National Park, WY 82190
(307) 344-7311
44.735384, -110.487912

Bison

Day 9 *Activities*

HIKE: Devils Tower
1.7 mi 167' elv 0:45 EASY

The Tower Trail is a paved route that circumnavigates the basalt remains of an ancient volcano.

About .2 miles into the loop you will come to a side path that leads into the boulder field on the northwest side of the tower. The remainder of the loop is a stroll through stately ponderosa pine forests. Before reaching the northern extremity, the trail climbs steadily to a well placed bench before heading downhill and once again winding amongst boulders close to the base of the tower and returning to the trailhead.

Location
Devils Tower National Monument, Devils Tower, WY 82714
44.592730, -104.719978

Legend: Claw marks in the Rocks

The Lakota Tribe tells of a group of girls who while out playing where chased by a clan of enormous bears. With no escape in sight the girls prayed to the Great Spirit who made the rocks they where on lift into the sky out of the reach of the bears. But the bears where determined and dug their caws into the rock in attempt to climb it. The girls where safe as the rock lifted into the heavens and they were turned into the stars of the Pleiades constellation. But the claw marks of the frustrated bears remain to this day.

VIEW: Shell Falls

The falls and Shell Canyon are named for the many shell fossils found in the sedimentary canyon walls. Sixty million year ago, the area that is now the Bighorn Mountains began to bow up and the basin on either side began to sink. Over the past million years, Shell Creek has cut a deep chasm in the sedimentary stone and ancient granite.

Location
US-14, Shell, WY 82441
44.766579, -107.787872

	LOCATION	DISTANCE	TIME
🟢	Canyon Campground, WY	0 mi	0
🟢	Lookout Point, WY	2 mi	0:10
🟢	Artist Point, WY	4 mi	0:20
🔵	Norris Geyser Basin, WY	16 mi	0:45
🔵	Artist Paint-Pots, WY	21 mi	1:00
🟡	Gibbons Falls, WY	56 mi	2:30
🟡	Firehole River Swimming Area, WY	63 mi	2:45
🟠	Fountain Paint-Pots, WY	72 mi	2:50
🟣	Midway Geyser Basin - Grand Prismatic, WY	75 mi	3:00
🩷	Old Faithful Inn, WY	83 mi	3:15
	Total	83 mi	3:15

Lodging

Old Faithful Inn
3200 Old Faithful Inn Rd, Yellowstone, WY 82190
(307)344-7311
44.459923, -110.831213

Day 10 *Activities*

HIKE: Lookout Point - Red Rock Point
.7 mi 259' elv 0:30 EASY

These lookouts offer head on views of Lower Yellowstone Falls

From the parking area for Lookout Point on the North Rim Drive follow the paved trail towards Lookout Point until you reach the sign for Red Rock Point. The trail begins to switchback steeply into the canyon. Steps have been installed where needed and as you reach Red Rock Point a boardwalk has been installed that has many stairs which descend further into the canyon. At the end you are rewarded with a head on view of Lower Yellowstone Falls.

Location
44.7215071, -110.4877078

HIKE: Artist Point
.2 mi 16' elv 0:05 EASY

This is the quintessential viewpoint for the Grand Canyon of Yellowstone.

A short distance from the trailhead this paved trail will bring you to an overlook with panoramic views of the Grand Canyon of the Yellowstone River.

Location
44.7200744, -110.4798785

History: Explorers

John Colter, a member of the Lewis and Clark Expedition, went on a solo reconnaissance of the area and passed through a portion of what later became Yellowstone National Park. Cut off from the rest of the expedition by early snowfall, he was forced to spend the winter of 1807–1808 in what would become the northeastern section of the park near Tower Falls. When he made it to civilization in 1809 he told his story, what people considered tall tales, describing the boiling landscapes.

In 1856 Jim Bridger returned from an excursion into the area with reports of boiling springs, spouting water, and a mountain of glass and yellow rock. His report where ignored due to his reputation as a "spinner of yarns".

The Cook–Folsom–Peterson Expedition of 1869, was the first reputable survey of the area. The Folsom party followed the Yellowstone River to Yellowstone Lake. When they returned the tall tales of the area became a topic of magical realism that motivated the surveyor-general of Montana, Henry Washburn, to conduct an official U.S. Army survey of the area.

Grand Canyon of the Yellowstone

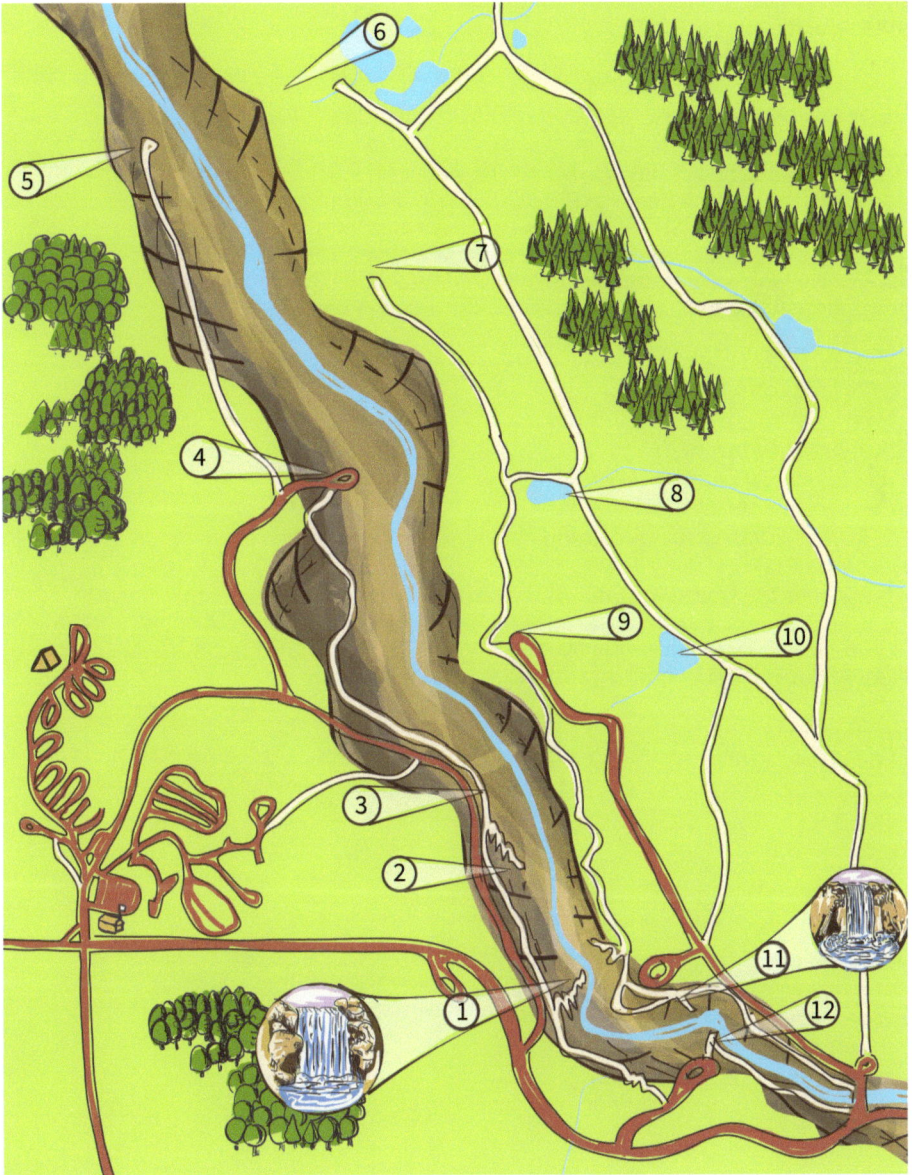

FEATURE

1. Brink of the Lower Falls
2. Lookout Point
3. Grand View
4. Inspiration Point
5. Cascade Overlook
6. Silver Cord Cascade
7. Point Sublime
8. Lily Pad Lake
9. Artist Point
10. Clear Lake
11. Upper Falls Viewpoint
12. Brink of the Upper Falls

Day 10 *Activities*

HIKE: Norris Geyser Basin
2.9 mi 180' elv 1:00 EASY

This is the the hottest and most dynamic thermal area in the park.

The trail begins by passing the Norris Geyser Basin Museum where the choice of starting with the Back Basin or Porcelain Basin sections is made. Starting with Back Basin go left towards Steamboat Geyser. Steamboat is the worlds tallest geyser but has infrequent eruptions often going months between activity. On the far end of Back Basin take a right onto a short out and back spur. Following the left split in the trail before its completion will take you to Porcelain Basin.

Location
44.7261147, -110.7016969

HIKE: Artist Paintpots
1 mi 101' elv :30 EASY

The hydrothermal area has colorful hot springs, mudpots, and small geysers.

After .3 mies the trail splits into the loop that navigates the best of the thermal features. Take a left to continue in a clockwise direction. This will bring you to Blood Geyser viewable from a scenic overlook. At the far end of the loop the trail descends one switchback to the boardwalk below.

Location
44.6963594, -110.7415790

FEATURE

1. Emerald Spring
2. Steamboat Geyser
3. Cistern Spring
4. Pit Black Spring
5. Echinus Geyser
6. Arch Steam Vent
7. Mystic Spring
8. Puff n' Stuff Geyser
9. Black Hermit Cauldron
10. Green Dragon Spring
11. Blue Mud Steam Vent
12. Yellow Funnel Spring
13. Pork chop Geyser
14. Pearl Geyser

Norris Geyser Basin

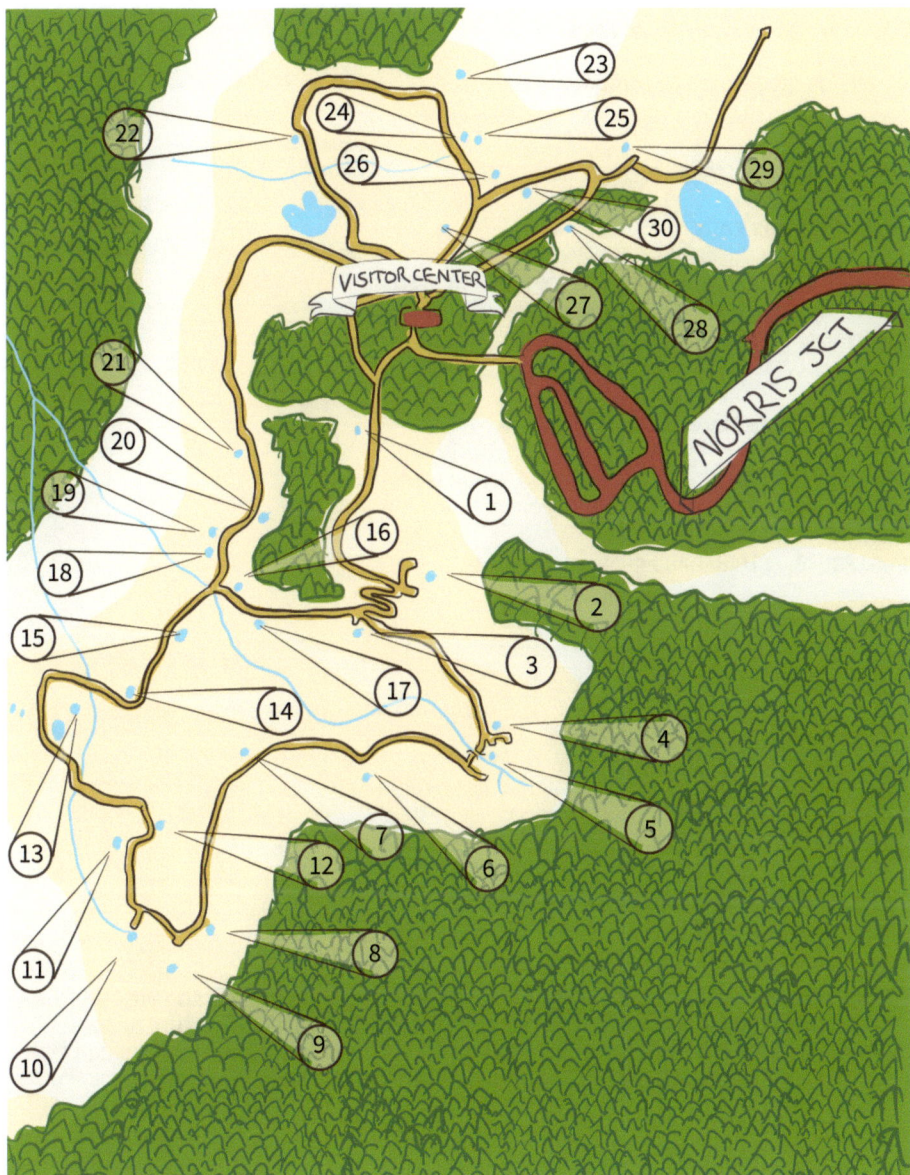

FEATURE

15. Vixen Geyser
16. Corporal Geyser
17. Veteran Geyser
18. Palpitator Spring
19. Fearless Geyser
20. Monarch Geyser Crater
21. Minute Geyser
22. Whales Mouth

23. Pinwheel Geyser
24. Whirling Geyser
25. Constant Geyser
26. Sunday Geyser
27. Ledge Geyser
28. Congress Pool
29. Porcelain Spring
30. Hurricane Vent

Day 10 *Activities*

COOK: Iron Springs Picnic Area

A riverside picnic area that is often overlooked

Location
44.6596664, -110.7682066

VIEW: Gibbons Falls

A beautiful waterfall visible from the parking area.

Location
44.6538606, -110.7715513

SWIM: Firehole River Swimming Area

The only official swimming area left in Yellowstone.

Location
44.6183973, -110.8604934

HIKE: Fountain Paint Pots
.7 mi 26' elv 0:30 EASY

Within this geothermal area, every type of thermal feature is represented.

Location
44.5478401, -110.8078798

HIKE: Grand Prismatic Boardwalk
.3 mi 10' elv 0:15 EASY

One of the most colorful geothermal features in the world.

The springs rainbow of colors gives it a surreal appearance that can be viewed from this short one-way boardwalk. The distinct rings of varying temperature allow different species of heat loving bacteria to inhabit the different zones. The high temperature in the center keep it a sterile blue color in its eye.

Location
44.5288469, -110.8360507

HIKE: Grand Prismatic Overlook
1.2 mi 105' elv 0:45 EASY

A view from above the Grand Prismatic Spring.

From the Fairy Falls Parking lot walk over the bridge across the Firehole River. In just over a half mile a left fork takes you to the overlook platform.

Location
44.5154043, -110.8323680

Midway Geyser Basin

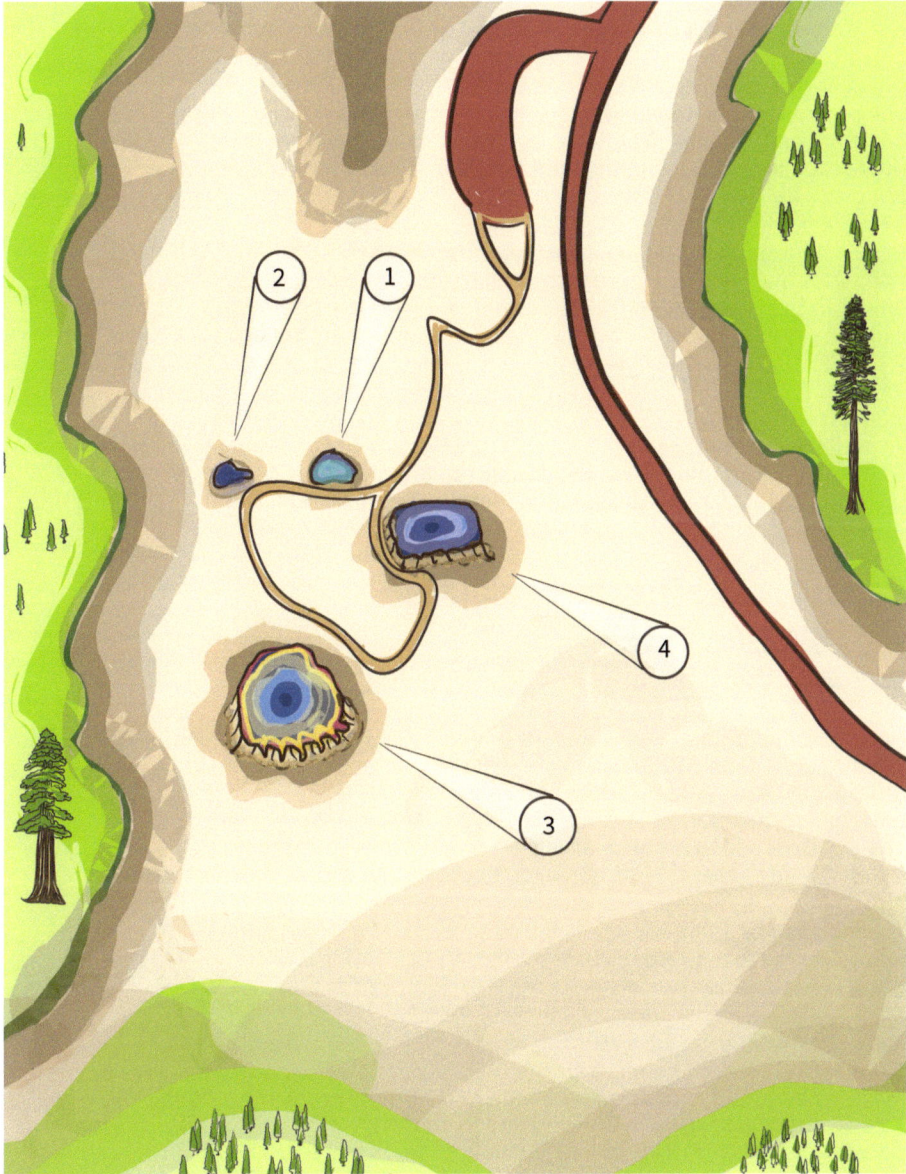

FEATURE

1. Turquoise Pool
2. Opal Pool
3. Grand Prismatic Spring
4. Excelsior Geyser Crater

Park History: Yellowstone National Park

Yellowstone National Park was established in 1872. It was the first National Park designated.

The original inhabitants of the area were the ancestors to contemporary Blackfeet, Cayuse, Coeur d'Alene, Nez Perce, and Shoshone. They kept the area a secret from the European settlers and most did not believe tales of the natural wonders of the area until the park was established.

Early park visitors would have enjoyed campfire discussions much like we do today. Behaviors that they exhibited that would not be permitted today included carving names in the travertine deposits, feeding bears, and even doing laundry in the Old Faithful geyser. Due to the observance of such disrespectful behavior the U.S. Army was sent to oversee the management of Yellowstone for 30 years between 1886 and 1916.

Visitation increased dramatically by the 1920s as more and more tourists began arriving by automobile. The Civilian Conservation Corps (CCC) projects in the 1930s built the majority of the early visitor centers, campgrounds, and the current system of park roads.

Parkitecture: The Old Faithful Inn

The Old Faithful Inn is a national historic landmark and the inspiration for modern "parkitecture."

Opened to the public in 1904 and, designed by architect Robert Reamer, Old Faithful Inn is a prime example of rustic craftsmanship, and is one of only a few remaining historic log hotels in the United States. Built from trees cut from the surrounding area, and stone quarried locally, the lodge is the largest log structure in the world. The Lodge provided quite luxurious accommodations for the time that included steam heating generated from nearby geothermal sources, and electric lights.

The initial construction is now referred to as the Old House, and included the grand lobby and the first group of guest rooms. The east wing was completed in 1914, and the west wing in 1927, bringing in the total footprint to almost 700 feet in length.

Early 20th Century visitors would have been primarily east coast elite who visited by traveling on the Northern Pacific Railroad which held the concession for operating lodging within the park. A journey from New York City took over a week and would have included a transfer in Chicago and Minnesota before getting on a direct line to Gardner Montana. A stage coach journey was required to get from Gardner to the Lodge.

The Old Faithful Inn was placed on the National Register of Historic Places on July 23, 1973.

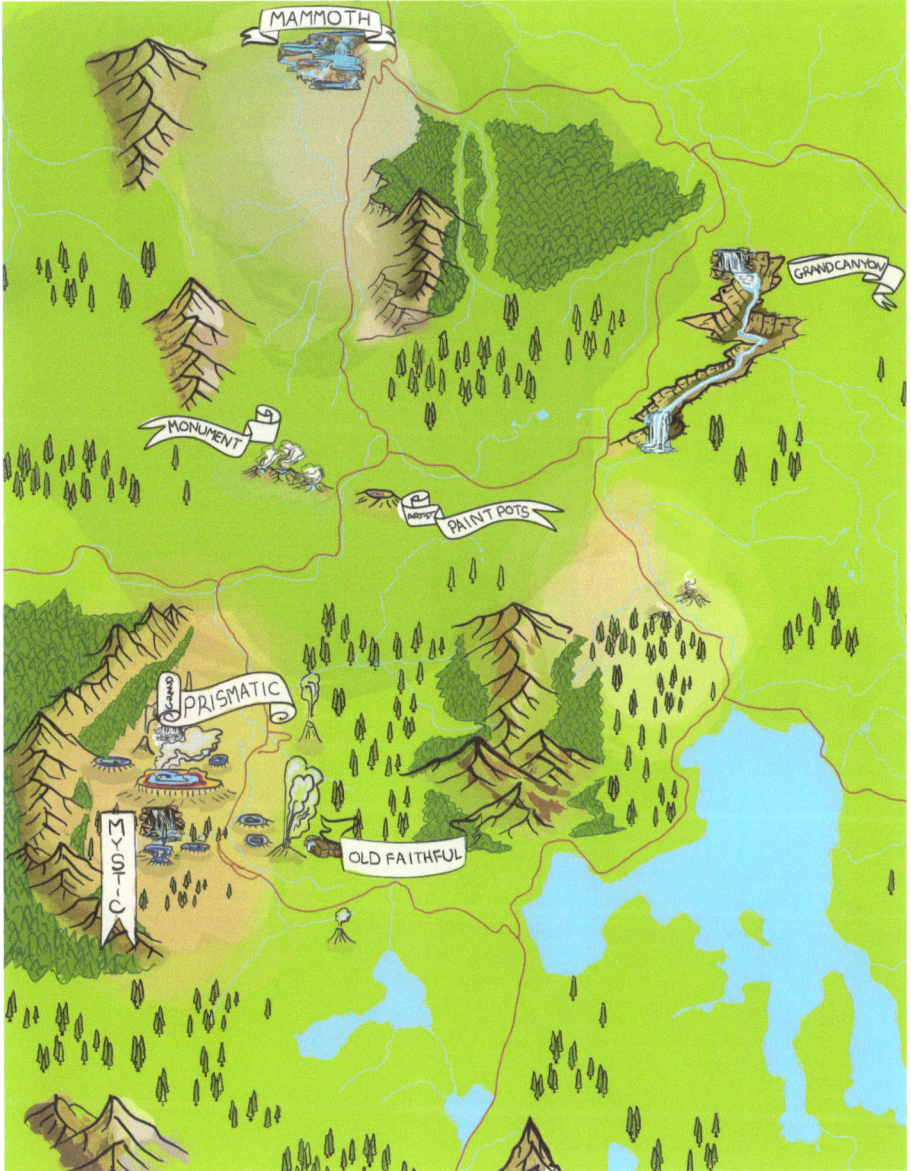

Lodging

Old Faithful Inn
3200 Old Faithful Inn Rd, Yellowstone, WY 82190
(307)344-7311
44.459923, -110.831213

Upper Geyser Basin

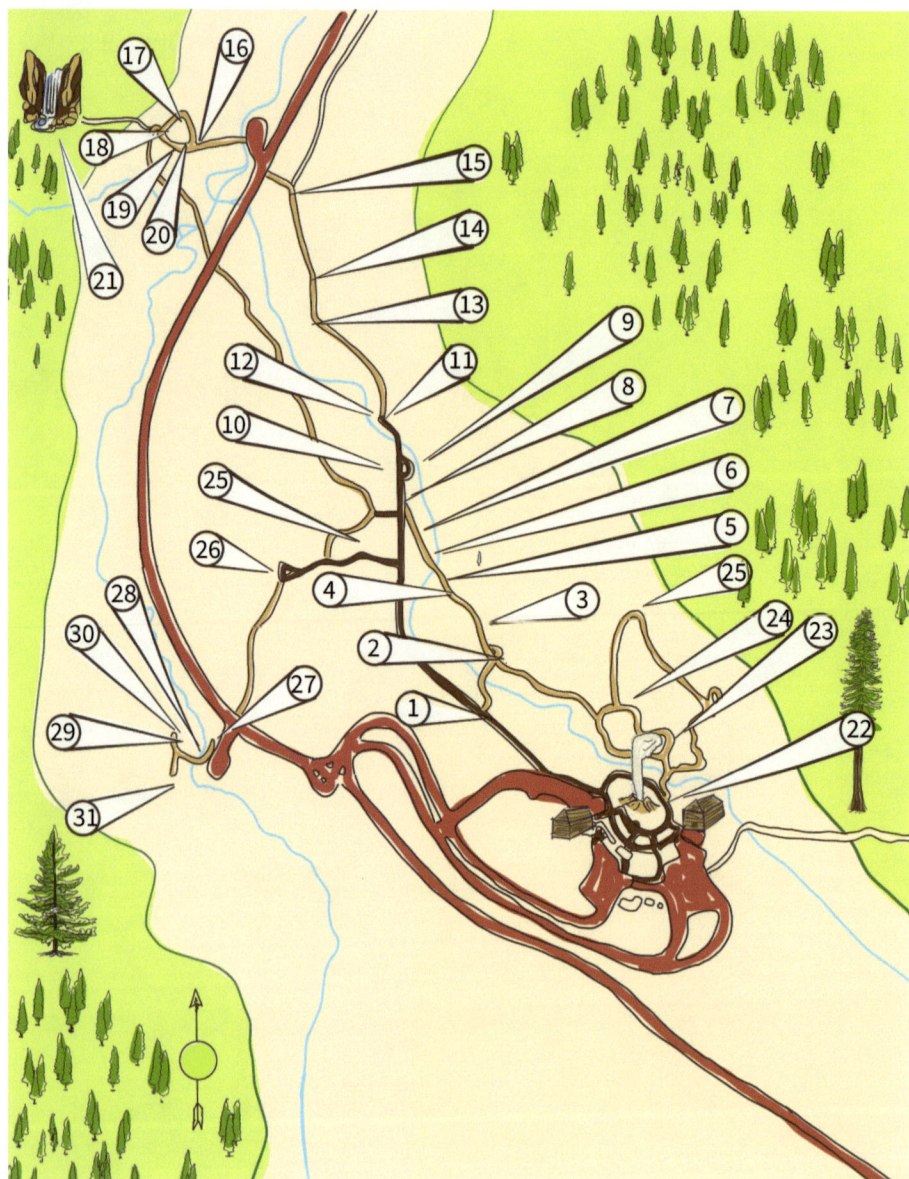

FEATURE

1. Castle Geyser
2. Spasmodic Geyser
3. Grand Geyser
4. Beauty Pool
5. Chromatic Pool
6. Oblong Geyser
7. Giant Geyser
8. Grotto Geyser

9. Riverside Geyser
10. Chain Lakes
11. Spiteful Geyser
12. Morning Glory Pools
13. Artemis Geyser
14. Gem Pool
15. Mirror Pool
16. Sapphire Pool

Day 11 *Activities*

HIKE: Mystic Falls and Upper Geyser Basin from Old Faithful
7 mi 190' elv 3:45 MODERATE

This half day activity visits the Upper Geyser Basin and Mystic Falls.

From the Old Faithful Inn take a left on the Upper Geyser Basin Trail until you reach the junction near Castle Geyser at .3 miles. To the right is the UGB-Biscuit Basin trail you will be returning on. Keep straight on Watertown Valley to the intersection with the Black Sand Basin Trail at .9 miles. The intersection with UGB trail will be reached at 1 mile. Take a left heading towards Black Sand Basin then in less than a tenth of a mile take a right on UGB-Biscuit Basin Trail. Cross route 191 at the 2 mile mark and soon you will cross the Little Firehole River and at 2.4 miles you will reach the trailhead for Mystic Falls. At 2.7 miles you will reach the intersection with the Fairy Creek Trail. Take a left and continue to Mystic Falls at 3.2 miles. Take a break before heading back to the Mystic Falls Trailhead. BISCUIT BASIN WAS CLOSED IN 2024 due to eruptions that destroyed the boardwalk. If its open you can continue through Biscuit basin to the Artemis Trailhead. If still closed follow the route you came in on to Route 191 and take a left at 4.5 miles and follow the road a quarter of a mile to the Artemis Trailhead and take a right onto the UGB Biscuit basin east side trail. Take another right at the intersection with the Power Line trail. You will pass many hydrothermal features and cross the Firehole River at 5.7 miles. There are pit toilets just after the crossing on the Riverside Geyser spur. At 5.8 miles, just before the junction where you headed towards Black Sand Basin take a left onto the Upper Geyser Basin Trail. Cross the Firehole River at 6 miles. At 6.4 miles take a right to stay on the UGB trail. Cross the Firehole River and take a left onto the UGB - Biscuit Basin trail that you came in on. You will arrive back at the Old Faithful Inn at the 7 mile mark.

Location
Starts at the Old Faithful Inn.

Feature	Distance	Time
Trailhead	0.0	0:00
Trail Junction UGB - Biscuit Basin (west)	1.0	0:30
Route 191	2.0	1:00
Mystic Falls Trailhead	2.4	1:15
Mystic Falls	3.2	1:45
Route 191	4.5	2:30
Riverside Geyser	5.7	3:00
Upper Geyser Basin (east) Junction	6.4	3:15
Old Faithful Inn	7.0	3:45

FEATURE

17. Mustang Spring
18. Avaco Spring
19. Shell Geyser
20. Jewel Geyser
21. Mystic Falls
22. Old Faithful
23. Giantess Geyser
24. Autumn Geyser
25. Solitary Geyser
26. Punch Bowl Spring
27. Opalescent Pool
28. Cliff Geyser
29. Rainbow Pool
30. Sunset Lake
31. Emerald Pool

HIKE: Solitary Geyser - Old Faithful Overlook Loop
2.5 mi 175' elv 1:00 EASY

Follow the Observation Point Trail clockwise to Solitary Geyser then on to Observation point to the overlook of Old Faithful.

Location
Starts at the Old Faithful Inn.

HIKE: Black Sand Basin via Daisy Geyser
4 mi 30' elv 1:30 EASY

This trail can be added onto the Mystic falls hike or done as a separate hike. The first mile is the same as the Mystic Falls hike.

Start on UGB-Biscuit Basin trail to Daisy Geyser Loop and proceed west on Punchbowl - Black Sand Basin trail. Cross route 286 and walk past parking lot to enter the loop. Return as you came

Location
Starts at the Old Faithful Inn.

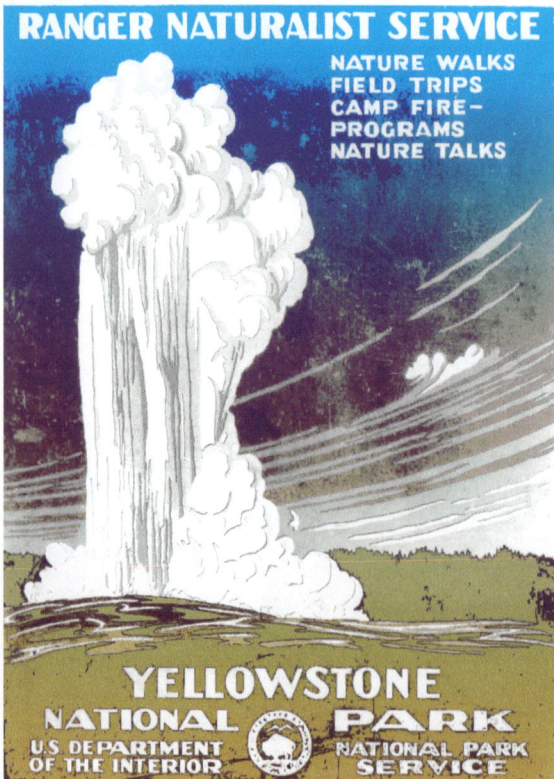

Colorized b&w negative scan originally designed by Works Progress Administration artist C. Don Powell 1938

Day 12

Yellowstone National Park, WY - Glacier National Park, MT

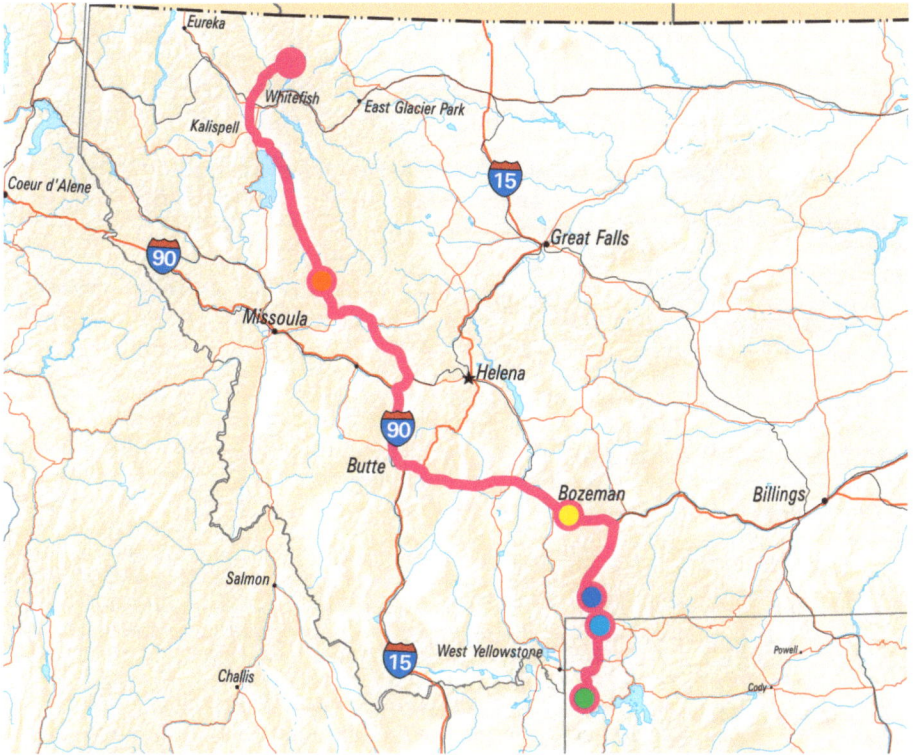

LOCATION	DISTANCE	TIME
Old Faithful Inn, WY	0 mi	0:00
Mammoth Hot Springs, WY	51 mi	1:20
Yellowstone Hot Springs, MT	75 mi	2:00
Bozeman Resupply, MT	150 mi	3:20
James Girard Memorial Grove, MT	375 mi	7:00
Avalanche Creek Campground, MT	505 mi	9:15
Total	505 mi	9:15

Grizzly Bear

Campground

Avalanche Campground
West Glacier, MT 59936
(406) 888-7800
48.676546, -113.818525

Day 12 *Activities*

HIKE: Mammoth Hot Spring
2.7 mi 383' elv 1:00 EASY

Countless travertine terraces dripping with hot water from the many thermal sources.

Mammoth Hot Spring has two primary areas, the upper and lower terraces, that can be combined for a larger loop. The Lower Terrace is the recommended starting point. It is a boardwalk trail with several hundred stairs. One of the unique features found here is the tower named Liberty Cap. It is the travertine terraces of built up mineral deposits that make this area so striking. From the upper terraces one is also afforded views of Montana's Rocky Mountains.

This area is also the location of the Horace M. Albright Visitors Center that was once home to the U.S. Calvary that guarded the park.

Location
44.9741230, -110.7042331

SOAK: Yellowstone Hot Spring

This developed hot spring features many cement pools of varying temperature that can be soaked in for a fee.

In 1909 a sanitarium facility and the Corwin Springs Hotel were built on what is now the site of the Yellowstone Hot Springs. Next to the hotel they built a large enclosed swimming pool with hot water transported to the pool through wooden pipes from the LaDuke Hot Springs two miles upstream. These mineral hot springs became a hot spot for early medical tourism. The hotel burned down in 1916 and the facility was abandoned until the mineral pools were rebuilt in 2018.

Location
45.1136554, -110.7928305

VIEW: James Girard Memorial Grove

Visit a 1,000 year old Tamarack Tree.

Just outside of Seeley Lake off of Boy Scout Road can be found the worlds oldest and largest Western Larch (Tamarack) tree named Gus. Gus is over 1,000 years old. This is not a well developed area so keep an eye out for the trailhead.

Location
47.1842836, -113.5208437

Mammoth Hot Springs

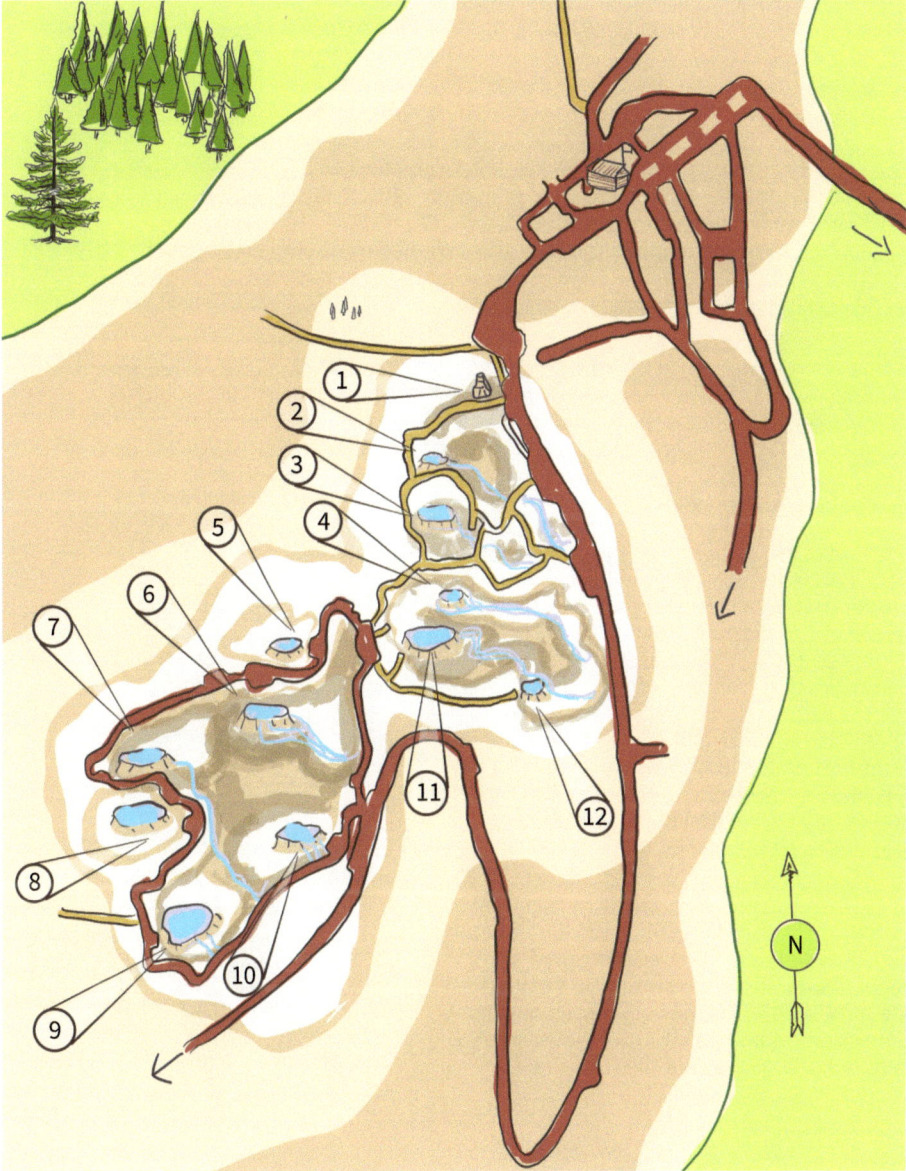

FEATURE

1. Liberty Cap
2. Pallette Spring
3. Minerva Terrace
4. Cleopatra Terrace
5. Prospect Terrace
6. New Highland Terrace
7. Orange Mound Spring
8. Bath Lake
9. White Elephant Back Terrace
10. Angel Terrace
11. Main Terrace
12. Canary Spring

Mammoth Hot Springs Historic District

Since the parks establishment in 1872, the Mammoth Hot Springs area has served as the gateway to Yellowstone.

Roosevelt Arch, 1903

The road from the park's boundary in Gardiner, Montana, to its headquarters at Mammoth Hot Springs, Wyoming, was built in 1884. The arch constructed over the road became known as Roosevelt Arch when President Theodore Roosevelt, who was vacationing in the park, spoke at the cornerstone laying ceremony in 1903.

Mammoth Post Office, 1938

Yellowstone's main post office was one of 1,007 post offices constructed from 1935 to 1938 "with a view to relieving countrywide unemployment." Most of these depression era work project structures still stand today as a testament to the progress that our country made during one of it's most challenging decades.

Fort Yellowstone, 1890 - 1900

Soon after the designation of Yellowstone National Park it became obvious that without proper management, the park would not be preserved as was intended in its foundation. Poachers and tourists posed a threat with behaviors that quickly reduced the animal population and left noticeable scars on the once pristine landscape. The United States Army was called in to protect the park from misuse. 35 structures remain from the 1890s and early 1900s when the US Army administered the park.

In 1910, at the height of the Army's presence in Yellowstone, there were 324 soldiers stationed here. These troops staffed not only Fort Yellowstone, but were stationed throughout the park in small details at various outposts. Conservation policies that were developed here led to the origin of the National Park Service.

By 1916, the National Park Service was established and the US Army moved out. It is this origin with the United States Army that influenced the Park Ranger uniform that is still present today with its signature flat brimmed calvary hat.

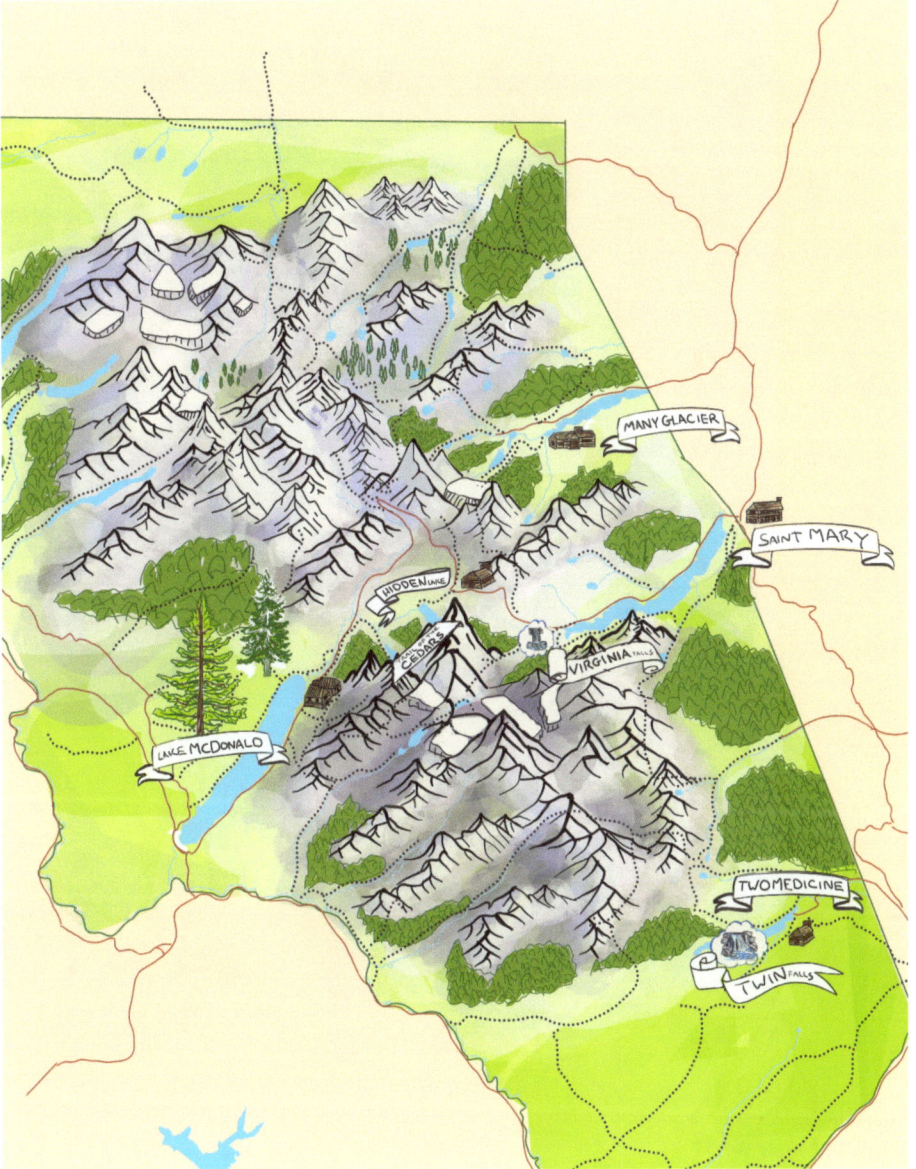

Campground

Avalanche Campground
West Glacier, MT 59936
(406) 888-7800
48.676546, -113.818525

Avalanche Lake

FEATURE
1. Trail of the Cedars
2. Avalanche Gorge
3. Lake McDonald Junction
4. Avalanche Beach
5. Trails End

Day 13 *Activities*

HIKE: Avalanche Lake
6.4 mi 757 elv 3:30 EASY

Entering into a forest reminiscent of the Pacific Northwest this trail takes you along a pristine creek fed by glacial waters as it makes its way to Avalanche Lake.

The trail to Avalanche Lake begins with the Trail of the Cedar loop trail. The northern side of the boardwalk is more scenic and passes through an ancient forest of western hemlock and red cedar trees that are more than 500 years old. In .8 miles a footbridge spans Avalanche Creek providing a excellent view of the lower Avalanche Gorge. Just past the footbridge is the Avalanche Lake trail junction. After taking a left the trail begins to climb into dense forest. At one mile from the campground the trail arrives again at the banks of the creek with up-close views of the narrow gorge. Just beyond the 1 mile mark the trail leaves sight of the creek but continues in ear-shot to the lake. At 2.5 miles the north shore outlet of Avalanche Lake is obtained and hikers are rewarded with a small beach. There is a pit toilet located just before at the end of the trail at the north shore. Many waterfalls descend from Sperry Glacier in the distance. For more solitude one can continue another .75 miles along the western shoreline to the southern shore at the head of the lake.

Feature	Distance	Time
Trailhead	0.0	0:00
Avalanche Gorge	1.0	0:45
Avalanche Lake North Shore	2.5	1:30
Avalanche Lake South Shore	3.2	2:00

Location
Starts at Avalanche Campground.

Avalanche Lake

Day 13 *Activities*

VISIT: Lake McDonald Lodge

Located on the shore of Lake McDonald, this historic lodge seems frozen in time.

In addition to lodging, the facility offers dining, Red Bus tours up Going-to-the-Sun Road, and boat trips on the lake directly behind the lodge. Be sure to make reservations as these activities book up well in advance.

Location
48.6170103, -113.8780771

Parkitecture: Lake McDonald Lodge

This classic Swiss chalet style lodge is nestled on the shores of the largest lake inside the park.

Opened in 1914, and originally called the Lewis Glacier Hotel, the lodge was contracted by the prospector John E. Lewis who anticipated an influx of travel from the nearby Great Northern rail line. Designed by architect Kirtland Kelsey Cutter, Lake McDonald Lodge resemble a gorgeous Swiss chalet. Decorated in a hunting lodge style and adorned with Native American crafts, the lodge offered a rustic retreat to the mostly city slicker visitors.

Many of the original furnishings have remained in the lodge to this day, including the hickory chairs with log frames and the piano. Other furnishings are reproductions of Old Hickory and Roycroft pieces. The rugs are reproductions of the Gustav Stickley originals. The hanging lanterns are reproductions of original work made by Kanai craftsmen for the Prince of Wales Hotel in Waterton Lakes National Park, Canada.

The Lake McDonald Lodge was designated a National Historic Landmark in 1987.

Day 14
Glacier National Park, MT

LOCATION	DISTANCE	TIME
🟢 Avalanche Creek Campground, MT	0 mi	0:00
🔵 Logan Pass Visitors Center, MT	16 mi	0:40
🔵 Jackson Glacier Overlook, MT	19 mi	0:50
🟡 Wild Goose Island Viewpoint, MT	25 mi	1:05
🔴 Two Medicine Campground, MT	75 mi	2:10
Total	75 mi	2:10

Campground

Two Medicine Campground
East Glacier Park, MT 59434
(406) 888-7800
48.4908654, -113.3631064

Bighorn Sheep

Hidden Lake

FEATURE
1. Logan Pass Visitors Center
2. Hidden Lake Overlook
3. Hidden Lake
4. Clements Mountain
5. Avalanche Lake

Day 14 *Activities*

HIKE: Hidden Lake
5 mi 1,338' elv 3:30 MODERATE

Hidden Lake is perched high amongst the alpine gardens beside the going to the sun road.

The hike to Hidden Lake begins from the west side of the Logan Pass Visitors Center. From the back of the visitors center climb the staircase and stay to the right to arrive at the hanging gardens trailhead. The hike begins as a paved walkway through open meadows and soon transitions to boardwalk above the fragile wildflowers. Dominating the landscape is Clements Mountain an enormous exposed conical slab of granite. A little more than half a mile, after climbing a series of wooden stairs, the end of the boardwalk is reached. After just over a mile a small rise will be reached and a couple of small ponds will be passed. Between these two ponds is an unmarked trail that leads to Dragons Tail and good views of Hidden Lake. At 1.4 miles the official overlook is reached. Soon after the overlook, the trail begins to descend more and more rapidly and eventually reaches a series of switchbacks that bring you to the northwest corner of Hidden Lake. There is a pit toilet located at the end of the trail. A small beach extends in both directions and following the shore can bring you to more secluded viewpoints.

Feature	Distance	Time
Logan Pass Visitors Center	0.0	0:00
Overlook	1.3	0:45
Hidden Lake	2.5	1:30

Location
48.6954136, -113.7170550

Hidden Lake

Park History: Glacier National Park

Glacier National Park was established in 1910. It was the tenth National Park designated.

The area that is now Glacier National Park was once the dominion of the Blackfeet tribe in the east and the Flathead tribe to the west. To the Blackfeet, the mountains of this area, especially Chief Mountain and Two Medicine, were referred to as the "Backbone of the World" and were visited often for vision quests. Under pressure from the United States government, the Blackfeet gave up the mountainous areas of their land in 1895 to the government for designation as a wilderness preserve which later became part of the National Park.

European explorers came to this area searching for beaver and other animal pelts. Explorers were soon followed by miners and homesteaders. By 1891, the completion of the Great Northern Railway opened the area to tourists looking to experience the natural wonders. In 1900 the area was designated as a wilderness preserve but was still open to mining, logging, and homesteading. Influential leaders such as George Bird Grinnell, lobbied for the creation of a national park in order to preserve this natural wonder.

History: The Vision Quest

Young Blackfeet must perform a coming of age ritual by undertaking a quest for a vision in the solitude of the mountains.

The vision quest begins when a young Blackfeet's decides to go on his journey after receiving a dream that calls him to the mountains. In order to prepare for the journey the youth must undergo a purification ceremony where he sweats for four consecutive days. The young seeker of visions takes along tribal helpers to prepare a sweat lodge by gathering and heating rocks that are placed inside an earthen alcove covered in animal skins. After the purification ceremony is complete, the seeker finds a suitable place, high in the mountains isolated from others, to spend four days and four nights waiting for his vision. The vision usually comes in the form of an animal or spirit helper who teaches the seeker a power song. After learning his power song the young Blackfeet returns to his tribe knowing his purpose. With purpose the boy has become a man.

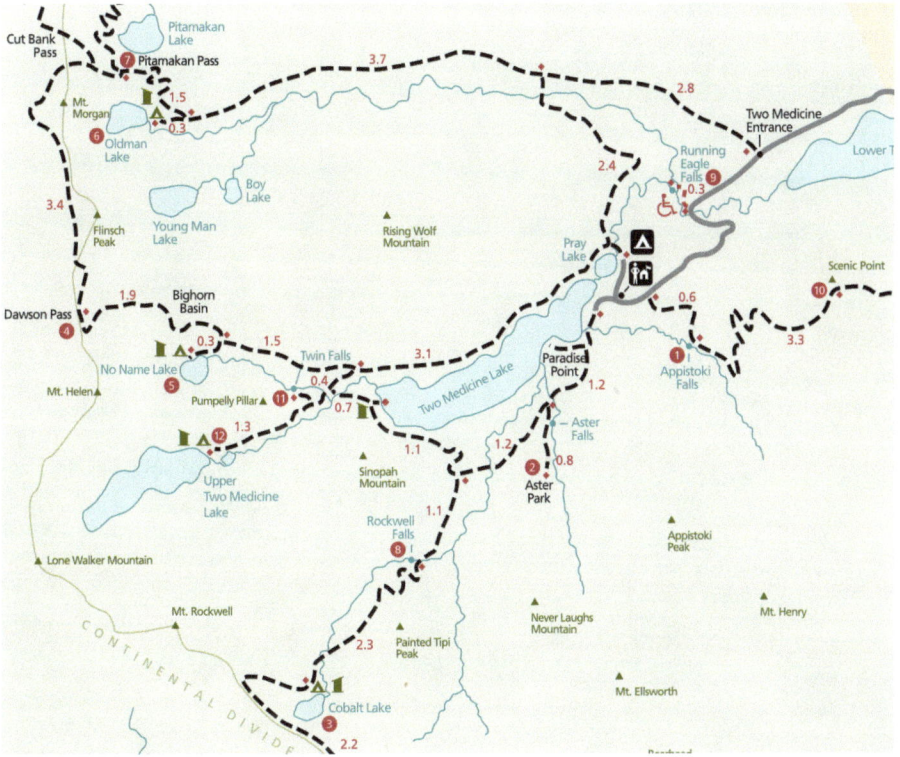

Two Medicine: Backbone of the World

"The Badger-Two Medicine is a place of power known to our people as Miistakis, the 'Backbone of the World.' Our people communicate with the Creator and find healing in the Badger-Two Medicine. The Blackfeet Nation has fought for generations to protect this place where our people can speak to Creator Sun while standing on Mother Earth,"

- Blackfeet Tribal Council Member Patrick Armstrong

Campground

Two Medicine Campground
East Glacier Park, MT 59434
(406) 888-7800
48.4908654, -113.3631064

Mountain Goat

Two Medicine

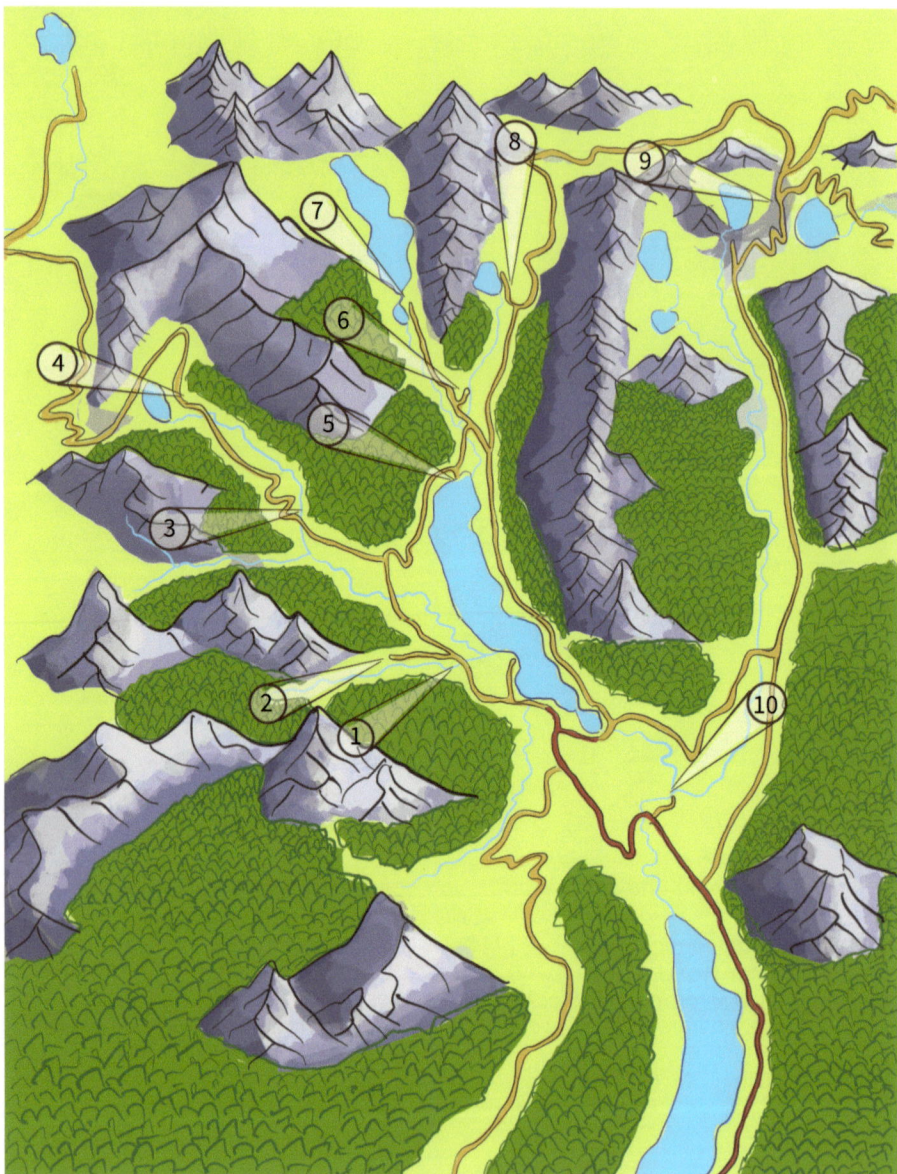

FEATURE

1. Aster Creek
2. Aster Falls
3. Rockwell Falls
4. Cobalt Lake
5. Ferry Dock
6. Twin Falls
7. Upper Two Medicine Lake
8. No Name Lake
9. Oldman Lake
10. Running Eagle Falls

Day 15 *Activities*

HIKE: Cobalt Lake
10.8 mi 1557 elv 6:15 MODERATE

Cobalt Lake is the lesser visited option from Two Medicine that passes not one but two spectacular waterfalls along the way. Although long in distance this hikes elevation gain is spread out so it is not particularly strenuous. The steepest section is between Rockwell Falls and Cobalt Lake. Pack a lunch, this hike is going to take all day.

South Shore Trailhead is .6 miles from Two Medicine Campground. Less than a mile into the hike is a spur trail that goes to Paradise Point, a small beach area with excellent views of the lake. At 1.8 miles Aster Creek is crossed and in a short distance after the crossing is the spur trail to Aster Falls. At 3.1 miles the suspension bridge over Paradise Creek is crossed. At 3.4 miles you will reach the junction with the South Shore Trail that leads to the boat dock where a boat shuttle can be arranged for your return trip to shorten the hike if desired. To continue to Cobalt Lake take a left and at 4 miles cross another footbridge and soon you will arrive at Rockwell Falls. Once past the falls the trail begins to climb a series of switchbacks. As you climb higher the trail reaches the subalpine zone full of meadows and dwarf trees. At 6.4 miles the trail reaches its high point and descends to the shores of Cobalt Lake. On the way back the South Shore trail junction is reached at 9.4 miles. To take the boat shuttle back (you must purchase tickets in advance) take a left. At 10.8 miles you will reach the boat shuttle. CHECK SHUTTLE TIMES IN ADVANCE. Last boat back is usually at 5:15 pm but it is recommended that you make the earlier 3:15 shuttle since if the last boat is full you will have to walk back adding another 2 miles to the hike.

Feature	Distance	Time
Campground	0.0	0:00
Trailhead	0.6	0:30
Aster Falls	2.0	1:00
South Shore JCT	3.4	1:45
Rockwell Falls	4.2	2:30
Cobalt Lake	6.4	4:00
South Shore JCT	9.4	5:30
Boat Launch	10.8	6:15

Location
Starts at the Two Medicine Campground.

Legend: Old Man on a Raft

In the beginning, water was everywhere. Floating on the water was a raft, and on the raft was "Old Man" the Sun and all the animals.

Old Man wished to make land, and he told the beaver to dive to the bottom and bring up a little mud. The beaver dived into the water but could not reach the bottom. Then the loon tried, and after him, the otter, the water was too deep for them as well. At last, the muskrat was sent down. He was gone for so long that they thought he had drowned. But when he floated up to the surface looking dead, Old Man pulled him up on the raft and looked at his paws. On his paws he found a little mud. The muskrat lived and lives on in legend.

Old Man dried this mud, and scattered it over the water, and soon land was formed where all the animals could live.

-Blackfeet Creation Story

Colorized b&w negative scan originally designed by Works Progress Administration artist Unknown, 1939

LOCATION	DISTANCE	TIME
🟢 Two Medicine Campground, MT	0 mi	0:00
🔵 Missoula Resupply, MT	208 mi	4:00
🔴 Powell Campground, ID	258 mi	5:20
Total	258 mi	5:20

Campground

Powell Campground
Lolo, MT 59847
46.51226, -114.7172188

Moose

Day 16 *Activities*

RESUPPLY: Missoula Montana
Walmart Supercenter
3555 Mullan Rd, Missoula, MT 59808
46.8843853, -114.0419098

HIKE: Weir Creek Hot Springs
.7 mi 164' elv :30 EASY

An easy to reach hot spring that hangs on a hillside above a forested ravine.

The Trailhead is located near milepost 142 on the south side of the road. The trail begins with a moderate incline and gets steeper as it follows Weir Creek upstream. The main pool is on the top of the hill. There are 3 smaller pools located down the hillside overflow.

The main pool ranges in temperature between 100-104 degrees. The lower pools temperature varies based on air temperature since it does not have its own source.

Location
46.4581562, -115.0350637

Weir Creek Hot Springs

54

Day 17
Lolo Pass, ID

Campground

Powell Campground
Lolo, MT 59847
46.51226, -114.7172188

Jerry Johnson Hot Springs

FEATURE
1. Lower Pools
2. Middle Pools
3. Upper Pools

Day 17 *Activities*

HIKE: Jerry Johnson Hot Springs
2.6 mi 265' elv 1:00 EASY

One of the most rewarding hot spring destinations available without much effort.

The Warm Spring Trailhead is located just across the bridge at mile marker 152. An easy mile of walking will bring you to the lower source that is hidden from view in the river bed below. Another half mile will bring you to the middle and upper sources which are visible from the trail.

The lower pools are are fed from a waterfall source that is 115 degrees and soaking temperatures range from 95-100 degrees. Due to there location on the river they may be under water in times of high flow. There is a hot waterfall that feeds into the lowermost pool.

The middle pools are located just upstream from the waterfall pool near a large boulder on the rivers edge and temperatures range from 95-100 degrees. They may also be inundated with river water at times of high flow. They are more accessible and tend to be the most popular.

The upper pools are further up the trail, surrounded by forest, and offer more solitude. Temperatures range between 100-104 degrees.

Location
46.4753413, -114.8852395

K'useyneisskit: Road to the Buffalo

The route over the Bitterroot Mountains, known today as the Lolo Trail, has been used by the Nez Perce since they first occupied the area. Extending from Weippe Prairie to Lolo Pass Idaho, it was the main route over the Bitterroot Mountains to get from Idaho to western Montana and the northern Great Plains. The route was essential to the nomadic tribes since it provided access to hunting and fishing grounds and served as a trade route with other tribes.

Hah-hahts: The Grizzly Bear

A young boy was lost in the mountains. He was approached by Hah-hahts, the grizzly bear, angry that the humans were taking over his land. When confronted, the boy said, "I can only die. Death is only part of life. I am not afraid." The grizzly, impressed with his bravery, took the boy to the "backbone of the highest mountains" to show him where the quas-peet-za (curled hairs) lived. He also showed the boy the huckleberry, chokecherry, and serviceberry. When they returned to the Kamiah valley, before leaving him, the bear said, "Here your people are living. Go tell them what you have learned about this great land, the food that has been provided for them, and the trail that will take them across the mountain."

- Nez Perce Oral Tradition published in The Lewiston Tribune June 28, 2003

Explorers: Lewis & Clark

The expedition to find passage from the Mississippi to the Pacific Ocean.

The Lewis and Clark Expedition proposed that they could find a route across the newly acquired western portion of America to the Pacific Ocean. After acquiring the Pacific Northwest from France in the Louisiana Purchase, the United States needed to survey this new territory. The expedition was lead by Captain Meriwether Lewis and Second Lieutenant William Clark of the U.S. Army and was composed of military and civilian volunteers. The expedition left from Camp Dubois, Illinois, on May 14, 1804, and went up the Missouri River. They followed the tributaries of the Missouri until water passage was not possible. Now traveling on land, the expedition crossed the Continental Divide and descended the mountains of present day Idaho to the Columbia River. They followed the Columbia river west and reached the Pacific Ocean in 1805.

Along the way, the expedition enjoyed the Lolo Hot Springs in Idaho before making their way across the final mountain pass where the rivers began to flow West.

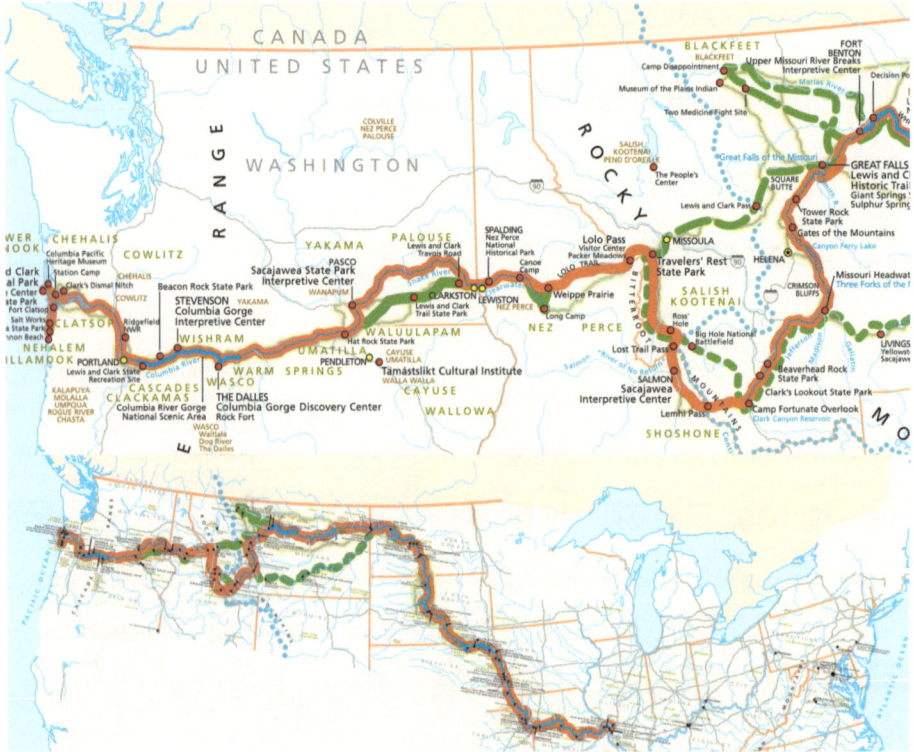

Day 18

LOCATION	DISTANCE	TIME
● Powell Campground, ID	0 mi	0:00
● Nez Perce National Historical Park, ID	153 mi	3:00
● Palouse Falls State Park, WA	240 mi	4:40
● Boulder Cave Picnic Area, WA	411 mi	7:40
● Paradise Inn, WA	455 mi	9:00
Total	455 mi	9:00

Lodging

Paradise Inn
52807 Skyline Trail, Paradise WA, 98368
(855)755-2275
46.7868811, -121.733936378837

Lynx

59

Day 18 *Activities*

LEARN: Nez Perce National Historical Park

The Visitors Center contains a small museum and store that sells locally made Native American crafts.

Location
46.4469402, -116.8244077

Chief Joseph & the Nez Perce

When Joseph became chief, he was under pressure to abandon his Wallowa land and relocate to a government mandated reservation near Lapwai, Idaho. Joseph had promised his father he would never leave their ancestral lands and refused. In 1877, the disputes between the tribal members and the United States turned violent and Joseph and other Nez Perce fled across the Bitterroot Mountains into Montana. After many battles they were taken to a reservation in Indian Territory, located in present day Oklahoma. They remained in Oklahoma until 1885 when they were sent to the Colville Reservation in North Central Washington.

VIEW: Palouse Falls State Park

The Palouse River drops 200' as it falls into a winding gorge of columnar basalt.

Location
46.6638242, -118.2282714

HIKE: Boulder Cave
1.5 mi 400' elv 1:00 EASY

Requires timed entry reservation that can be made 2-14 days in advance.

The trail to Boulder Cave was constructed in the 1930's by the Civilian Conservation Corps. A bridge over the Naches river and quick jaunt up the hill brings you to the entry of the cave. Bring a headlamp.

Location
46.9612428, -121.0852722

Lodging

Paradise Inn
52807 Skyline Trail, Paradise WA, 98368
(855)755-2275
46.7868811, -121.733936378837

Skyline Loop

FEATURE

1. Visitors Center
2. Myrtle Falls
3. Shuiskin Falls
4. Paradise Glacier
5. Panorama Point
6. Glacier Vista
7. Alta Vista

8. Moraine Trail
9. Nisqually Vista
10. Lakes Trail
11. Lakes Trail
12. Narada Falls
13. Reflection Lakes
14. Louis Lake

Day 19 *Activities*

HIKE: Skyline Loop
5.7 mi 1,778' elv 3:30 MODERATE

One of the most amazing alpine meadow destinations on Earth.

To hike in a counter-clockwise direction begin at the Visitor Center and follow the paved trail until you reach Myrtle Falls. Take the staircase down to the viewpoint to enjoy the falls. Just beyond the falls the trail will transition from pavement to dirt path. Stay to the right at a trail junction with the Golden Gate Trail and hike through forest before reaching the ridge-line. Once reaching the Stevens-Van Trump Monument snow may be encountered even into August. Past most of the snowfields the Golden Gate trail rejoins the Skyline Trail and the path becomes rocky and rugged as you climb to the highest point and best views on the loop and descend slightly to Panorama Point. From Panorama Point it is all downhill on the way back to the Visitor Center.

Location
Starts at the Paradise Inn.

The Staircase to Heaven

Carved into the steps that lead to the skyline trail from paradise are the following words:

"....the most luxuriant and the most extravagantly beautiful of all the alpine gardens I ever beheld in all my mountain-top wanderings...."

-John Muir, conservationist, 1889

What's in a name?

Denali was given back its original name in 2015 by executive order, so why not change Mount Rainier back to Tahoma?

George Vancouver named Mount Rainier in honor of his friend, Rear Admiral Peter Rainier during an expedition sailing the Puget Sound in 1792.

The common ancestral name of Mt. Rainier in Washington State is "Tahoma" for the Yakima Tribe or "təqʷuʔməʔ" for the Puyallup. This translates to "the mother of all waters"

According to Yakima legend, Tahoma is the place where during a great flood, the people and animals scrambled to the top of the peak and remaining there together until the waters subsided.

Efforts to restore the name to "Tahoma" have been around since the park was created. In 2009, the U.S. Board of Geographic Names rejected a petition to rename the mountain on the grounds that "the overwhelming support and the predominate use of the locals was for Mount Rainier." Another National Park in Alaska was first named Mount McKinley and had its name changed to Denali in 2015 on the grounds that Alaskan locals refused to call the mountain McKinley.

Park History: Mount Rainier National Park

Mount Rainier National Park was established in 1899. It was the fifth National Park to be designated.

The original inhabitants of the area were the ancestors of the Cowlitz, Muckleshoot, Nisqually, Puyallup, Squaxin Island, Yakama, and Coast Salish people.

Mount Rainier remained a remote and mostly inaccessible area up to its declaration as a National Park. During the first fifteen years of the park's existence with the absence of established regulations, mining, logging, and water management took their toll on the landscape. Congress passed legislation in 1908 preventing further mining claims within the park, and remaining claims were slowly bought back over the following decades. By 1911 roads had been constructed that let visitors deep into the park and the Paradise area was established as a camping and recreation area. By 1917 the Paradise Inn was completed bringing a level of comfort before unseen in the otherwise wild park.

Wonderland Trail

Though many user trails already existed within the parks boundaries, The newly designated National Park needed a more official travel network to patrol and protect the park's resources. The first sections of the Wonderland Trail were started in 1907, until the full loop of the mountain was completed in 1915.

Civilian Conservation Corps

President Roosevelt's "New Deal" brought funding that Mount Rainier needed for development. 1,000 men from the Civilian Conservation Corps (CCC) came each summer to work on trail construction, campground and road improvement. Many of the stone bridges and walkways were built by the CCC.

Parkitecture: Paradise Inn

A Swiss chalet styled lodge sits on the edge of the alpine meadows at Mount Rainier

Paradise Inn opened for business in 1917. It was the vision of the Park Service's first director Steven Mather. His intent was to provide an alternative to the rugged tent camps that existed at the time. Built under his watchful eye , the Inn was to be a model for other parks and paved the way to making the National Parks accessible to all fitness levels. The Inn brought a level of luxury to Mount Rainier that remained very active even through the Great Depression. But the Inn was expensive to maintain and the climate of its surroundings were brutal. In 2006 the Inn was closed to make seismic improvements and was reopened in 2008.

Day 20

Mount Rainier, WA - Staircase, WA

LOCATION	DISTANCE	TIME
Paradise Inn, WA	0 mi	0:00
Reflection Lake, WA	2 mi	0:07
Narada Falls, WA	3 mi	0:10
Olympia Resupply, WA	87 mi	2:10
Staircase Campground, WA	137 mi	3:00
Total	137 mi	3:00

Campground

Staircase Campground
NF-24, Hoodsport, WA 98548
(360) 565-3130
47.515373, -123.329668

Elk

65

Day 20 *Activities*

VIEW: Reflection Lake

A short distance from the parking lot is the best view of reflection lake with Mount Rainier in the distance.

Location
46.7685061, -121.7314463

WALK: Narada Falls

A series of ornate stone steps descends 100' to the viewpoint below.

Location
46.7751011, -121.7465645

RESUPPLY: Trader Joe's

Finally made it to a Trader Joe's

Location
1530 Black Lake Blvd SW Olympia, WA 98502
47.0331473, -122.9385597

HIKE: Staircase Rapids Loop
2.2 mi 190' elv 1:00 EASY

A short but rewarding hike through giant evergreen trees.

At the furthest point in the loop is a beautiful cascade and pool.

Location
Starts at the Staircase Campground.

History: Native Tribes

Eight Olympic Peninsula tribes recognize a relationship to the lands that are now the Olympic National Park. These tribes are the Lower Elwha Klallam, Jamestown S'Klallam, Port Gamble S'Klallam, Skokomish, Quinault, Hoh, Quileute, and Makah. The ancestors of the these tribes lived throughout the Olympic Peninsula, but ceded their lands and waters to the federal government via treaties in 1855 and 1856. These tribes now occupy reservations along the shores of the peninsula.

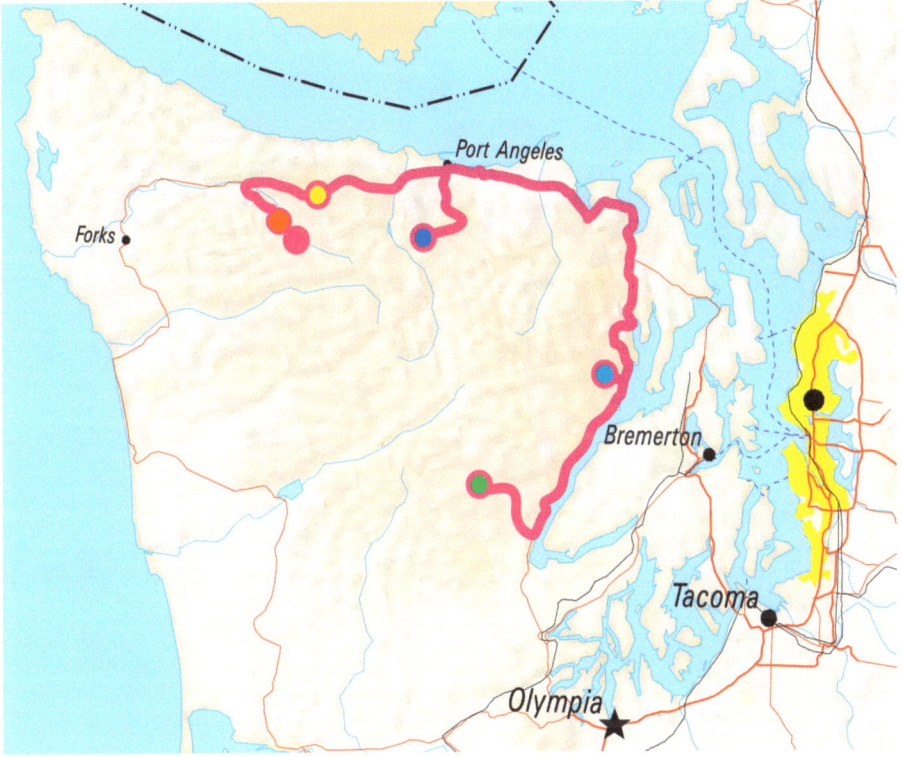

LOCATION	DISTANCE	TIME
🟢 Staircase Campground, WA	0 mi	0:00
🔵 Rocky Brook Falls, WA	45 mi	1:10
🔵 Hurricane Ridge, WA	123 mi	3:00
🟡 Marymere Falls, WA	163 mi	4:00
🟠 Ancient Groves Nature Trail, WA	180 mi	4:30
🔴 Sol Duc Resort, WA	184 mi	4:40
Total	184 mi	4:40

Lodging

Sol Duc Hot Springs Resort
12076 Sol Duc Hot Springs Rd. Port Angeles, WA
(360) 207-1258
47.9667528, -123.857825

Bobcat

Day 21 *Activities*

WALK: Rocky Brook Falls
.3 mi 32' elv :15 EASY

A short walk from the trailhead is one of the tallest and most spectacular falls on the peninsula.

Location
46.7751011, -121.7465645

HIKE: Hurricane ridge Cirque Rim Nature Trail
.8 mi 49' elv :20 EASY

Walk high atop the ridge line that extends from the heart of the Olympic Mountains.

This trail follows the rim of a large bowl as it arcs away from the former site of the now burned down Visitor Center.

Location
47.9700183, -123.4968374

HIKE: Marymere Falls
1.7 mi 314' elv 1:00 EASY

Waters fall down a moss covered cliff amidst an ancient old grove forest.

The trail leaves the parking area at Lake Crescent and meanders through majestic old growth forest on a relatively flat trail surrounded by mosses until it reaches the ravine that houses Marymere Falls. A short series of switchbacks with steps loops around the hillside affording views of the falls.

Location
48.0583948, -123.7879985

VISIT: Lake Crescent Lodge

On the south shore of Lake Crescent, is the historic Lake Crescent Lodge. The lodge was built in 1916. In 1937, President Franklin D. Roosevelt visited the Olympic Peninsula and stayed at the Lake Crescent Lodge. He would go on to sign into law the creation of Olympic National Park in 1938.

Location
48.0571850, -123.7991517

WALK: Ancient Groves Nature Trail
.5 0' elv :15 EASY

This oddly overlooked trail features old growth trees, mosses, and ferns similar to the western groves found in Olympic National Park but without the crowds.

Location
48.0037914, -123.9054441

Lodging

Sol Duc Hot Springs Resort
12076 Sol Duc Hot Springs Rd. Port Angeles, WA
(360) 207-1258
47.9667528, -123.857825

Sol Duc Falls

FEATURES
1. Sol Duc Hot Spring
2. Campground
3. Sol Duc Falls
4. Ancient Groves Nature Trail

Day 22 *Activities*

HIKE: Lover's Lane Sol Duc Falls Loop
5.8 mi 485' elv 3:00 MODERATE

Sol Duc Falls is a breathtaking waterfall that takes an off kilter descent through a winding chasm of moss covered rocks. The cascading water is surrounded by rainforest and empties into a turquoise basin. These falls are easily accessed via an easy nature trail, making them a popular destination for the many visitors that do not attempt this longer loop.

To complete this hike in a clockwise direction, start from the trailhead behind the resort, cross the river and walk upstream. Pass through the campground after the first mile. After the campground the trail gets steeper as it leaves the river and enters a primeval forest of hemlock, fir, and sitka spruce.

At the midway point in the loop, after a short steep climb, the falls become visible from a bridge located in a lush canyon of moss and fern covered rocks. Sol Duc Falls splits into as many as four different falls as it tumbles 45'. Various viewpoints are available in the surrounding area.

Crossing the bridge, the trail follows the other side of the river. This eastern side of the loop is much less traveled and affords a tranquil walk through old growth forest on the way back to the resort.

Location
Starts at the Sol Duc Resort.

Park History: Olympic National Park

Olympic National Park was established in 1938. It was the twenty-first National Park designated.

The original inhabitants of the Olympic Peninsula were the Hoh, Jamestown S'Klallam, Lower Elwha Klallam, Makah, Port Gamble S'Klallam, Quileute, Quinault and Skokomish tribes.

In 1889, an expedition led by Lt. Joseph P. O'Neil explored the rugged interior of the Olympic Mountains. O'Neil was so amazed by the landscape that he publicly advocated for the formation of a national park. In 1897 President Grover Cleveland designated the Olympic Forest Reserve to protect trees, but not the animals. Excessive hunting of elk led President Theodore Roosevelt to designate part of the Reserve as Mount Olympic National Monument to preserve the elk. President Franklin Roosevelt visited the Olympic National Monument and in 1938 signed an act establishing it as Olympic National Park. International recognition came in 1982 when UNESCO designated the Park as a World Heritage Site.

"Humankind has not woven the web of life. We are but one thread within it. Whatever we do to the web, we do to ourselves. All things are bound together. All things connect."

- Chief Seattle, Duwamish

71

Legend: The Olympic Dragons

The Native Americans of the region have passed down a creation story that explains the formation of the areas hot springs.

A long long time ago when the world was just beginning. There was a mountain bigger than all the rest. The mountains name was Olympus.

Mount Olympus had a wife Tahoma and they live together happily amongst the newly formed forest. But one day Olympus and Tahoma had the biggest fight the world had ever seen. The earth shook and the ground crumbled and Tahoma drifted off to a distant shore to be far far away from Olympus. With her departure Mount Olympus became very sad and lonely. In his loneliness mount Olympus decided that he needed companionship. So he conjured up two little creatures to be by his side. These creatures were like none that have ever been seen before. They had claws and wings. And Olympus called them dragons.

The two dragons were his companions and stayed below the earth in the caves of the mountain. Mount Olympus raised them as his sons and watched very very carefully that they did not wander out of the caves below the mountain. He noticed that they were eager to learn about the world beyond the caves but he could not let them wander out for they were growing bigger and bigger and would be a threat to all the little creatures that lived outside.

One day the littlest of the dragons Sol Duc told his brother Elwah it was very very important that they learn about this world outside. So the two brothers found the openings to the outer world and looked to see all of the beautiful creatures that live below. Each of them found a favorite spot one on each side of the giant ridge that led to the top of the mountain. Every day they snuck to their places and saw that so much was changing in the world outside. When they would return to the center of the mountain where they where allowed to play they would exchange stories about this world outside.

Mount Olympus overheard them exchanging stories and told them that they were never to venture outside of the caves and punished them for disobeying him. But no amount of punishment could keep them from wanting to explore.

On the darkest night of the year the two dragons decided to sneak out and to explore this wonderful world they had only seen from inside of the cave. It was so fascinating that they decided to stay even though they knew they would be punished severely by Mount Olympus when they returned. But what they did not anticipate was that without Mount Olympus to watch after them there was no food. So the two dragons began trying everything around to feed them. They discovered that almost everything was tasty and wondered why Mount Olympus had not permitted them to explore.

The two dragons made a pact that each would have his own side of the mountain and would not cross the ridge which divided the two sides. Each day they found something more and more delicious and soon there was almost nothing on the forest floor. They ate the trees they ate the animals and soon they flew about the sky to find the last of the creatures and ate the birds.

In their attempts to feed their appetite they began to compete and found it was harder and harder not to cross to the other side of the ridge which they agreed was the border of their feeding grounds.

Catching birds was very difficult, and in his attempt to catch one of the last remaining, Sol Duc crossed over to Elwah's side and met resistance from his brother.

Elwah chased Sol Duc to retrieve the last of the birds remaining. Neither of them could catch the bird but they soon began to fight amongst themselves. Both had grown very powerful and where able to spit fire at one another. As they spat at one another the last remaining grasses where set ablaze. Soon what remained of the forest was nothing but a scorched burnt pile of rocks.

The two dragons were exhausted from the fight and there was nothing left to eat but the one remaining bird which evaded them. They watched as this eagle carried its wings far away beyond the horizon of the world that they knew.

The dragons were tired and could not find the strength or the courage to go so far. There was nothing left for them to eat and they began to cry bitter hot tears. This was when they realized it was nothing left for them to do but to accept defeat. Each of the dragons Sol Duc and Elwah retreated to the caves from which they had emerged.

They had grown so large that they could hardly fit. The Dragon's squeezed and squeezed their giant bodies into the caves and as they squeezed the skin was pulled off of their flesh and blew all about the world around them.

The world slowly returned to life as the two dragons accepted their defeat in the caves beneath Olympus. In fact it flourished on their bitter hot tears which emanate to this day from the caves of Sol Duc and Elwah Hot Springs.

As humans emerged they found these places to be sacred and a place of negotiation between the native villages that grew all around. The waters are healing and so is the skin of the dragons which can be found all about the forest floor of the Olympic Peninsula.

The natives learned from the error of the dragons and kept peace and harmony amongst the forest and all the living things around.

We would be wise to listen to the story of the dragons for it is important not to disregard the rules that keep the balance of nature in order.

- This story was told to me by a ranger in the 90's and elaborated on over the years.

S'Klallam Totem Pole

Sol Duc, WA - Cape Disappointment, WA

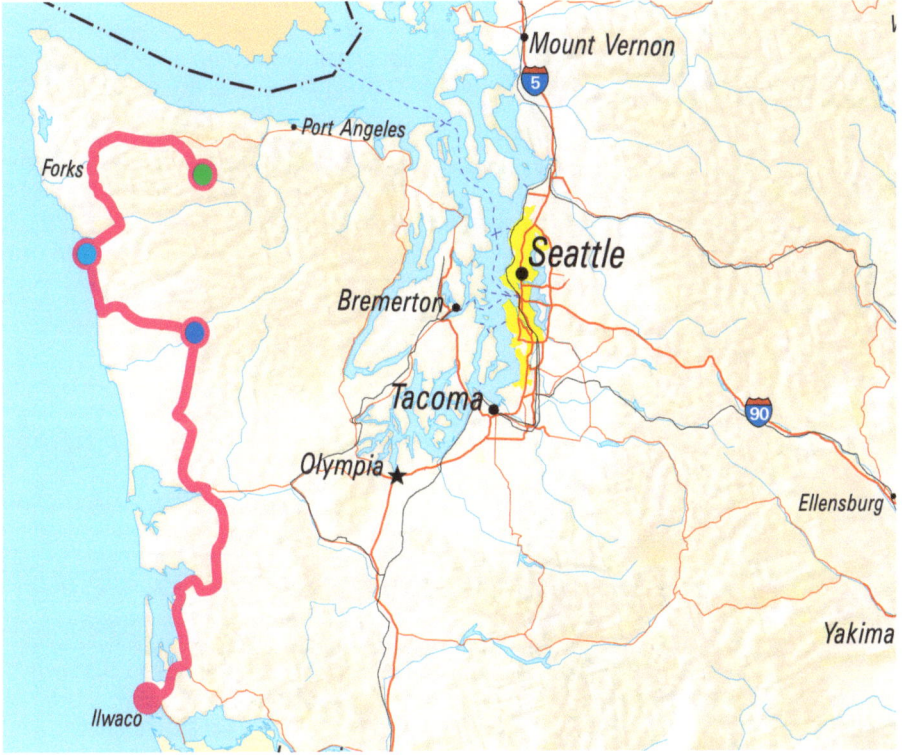

LOCATION	DISTANCE	TIME
🟢 Sol Duc Resort, WA	0 mi	0:00
🔵 Ruby Beach, WA	67 mi	1:30
🔵 Quinault Rainforest, WA	107 mi	2:15
🔴 Cape Disappointment, WA	221 mi	4:45
Total	221 mi	4:45

Campground

Cape Disappointment
244 Robert Gray Drive, Ilwaco, WA 98624
(360) 642-3078
46.28393364, -124.05463028

Otter

Day 23 *Activities*

HIKE: Ruby Beach
1 mi 49' elv :30 EASY

This beach is easily accessible and offers up a beautiful Pacific coastline with sea stacks and tide pools beneath a forested bluff that can be walked at low tide all the way to the Hoh River.

The trail switchbacks down a 50' tree covered bank to emerge at the ocean amongst a sea of driftwood. A trail has been cut through the giant sea logs that brings you to Cedar Creek. Follow the creek to its outlet at a sand beach. Cross the creek to get to the wider beach area and follow the shore to the tide pools around Abby Island. It is possible to head north along the beach another 2.5 miles to where the Hoh river collides with the Pacific Ocean.

Location
47.7099286, -124.4138069

HIKE: Quinault Loop
3.9 mi 364' elv 1:30 EASY

Here you can find an old growth forest that rivals the much busier Hoh. The loop here is also a much longer experience amongst the giants.

Starting at the Pacific Ranger Station follow the trail west along the lakefront. After 1 mile you will enter Willaby Campground and a short section of road walking will bring you to the parking area for the Rainforest Nature Loop. This section goes under the highway and follows a small creek. You can do the short loop or take a left to keep moving uphill. The trail moves up and down the ridge-line then enters a bog on a boardwalk. At the Falls Creek Junction there are two options. Go straight for a direct route to the lodge or turn right over the footbridge to complete the full loop. This adds another half mile to the journey but includes three additional bridges with babbling creeks before returning to the Pacific Ranger Station.

Location
47.4676143, -123.8475814

RELAX: Cape Disappointment Beach

Cape Disappointment is anything but what the name implies. Direct access to the beach from many of the campsites makes this a hidden gem.

There is accessible beach directly behind B loop or a short drive within the park will bring you to Waikiki Beach that features nice sand beaches beside sea-cliffs.

Location
Starts from Cape Disappointment Campground Loop B.

Day 24

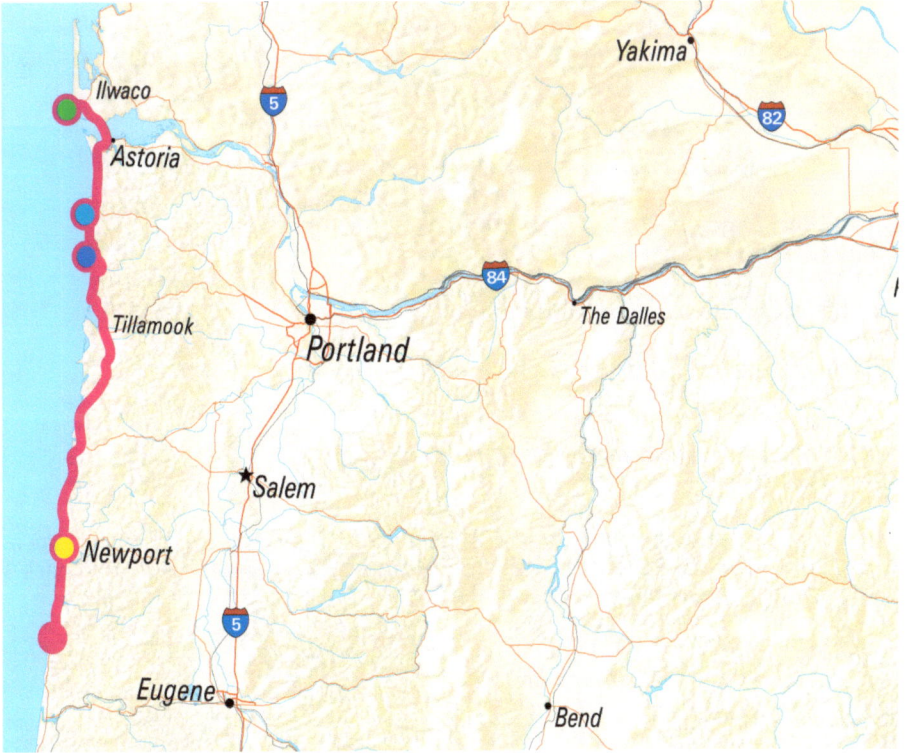

LOCATION	DISTANCE	TIME
🟢 Cape Disappointment, WA	0 mi	0:00
🔵 Crescent Beach, OR	40 mi	1:00
🔵 Short Sand Beach, OR	52 mi	1:20
🟡 RESUPPLY Newport, OR	150 mi	3:45
🔴 Cape Perpetua Campground, OR	180 mi	4:30
Total	180 mi	4:30

Campground

Cape Perpetua Campground
2200 Hwy 101 S Yachats, OR 97498
(541) 547-4580
44.2811111, -124.1002778

Great Horned Owl

Day 24 *Activities*

HIKE: Crescent Beach
.7 mi 187' elv :30 EASY

The trail starts at Ecola Point and meanders in a southernly direction up and down drainages in the bluff through a lush forest of sitka spruce. Descend a series of stairs to the beach.

Location
45.9193887, -123.9738451

HIKE: Short Sand Beach
1.2 mi 82' elv :30 EASY

Just before the beach is a nice picnic area with table.

Location
45.7614067, -123.9580569

HIKE: Devils Churn Restless way Captain Cook loop
1.8 mi 275' elv 1:00 EASY

Take the Giant Spruce Trail west towards the coast past the visitors center and take a right to Devil's Churn. Follow the Trail of the Restless Way to Devil's Churn and back along the coast where it meets up with the Captain Cook Trail to Thor's Well.

Location
Starts at Cape Perpetua Campground.

Cape Perpetua, OR - Gold Bluffs Beach, CA

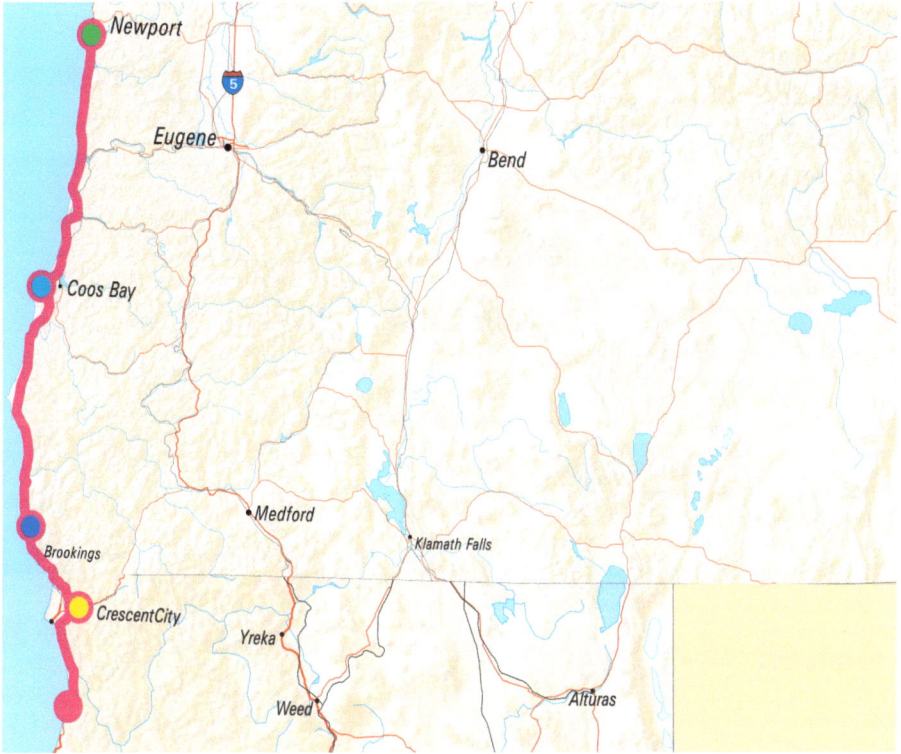

LOCATION	DISTANCE	TIME
🟢 Cape Perpetua, OR	0 mi	0:00
🔵 Cape Arago, OR	83 mi	1:50
🔵 Secret Beach, OR	181 mi	3:50
🟡 Stout Memorial Grove, CA	221 mi	4:30
🟡 Grove of the Titans, CA	223 mi	4:40
🟡 Boy Scout Tree, CA	224 mi	4:45
🔴 Big Trees, CA	258 mi	5:45
🔴 Gold Bluff Campground, CA	268 mi	6:15
Total	268 mi	6:15

Campground

Gold Bluffs Beach Campground
Davison Rd, Orick, CA 95555
(707) 465-7335
41.382217, -124.069882

White Tailed Deer

Day 25 *Activities*

HIKE: Cape Arago South Cove Trail
.3 mi 85' elv :20 EASY

A short trail leads down to a beach with excellent tide pools.

Location
43.3050193, -124.3983989

HIKE: Secret Beach
1.9 mi 406' elv 1:00 MODERATE

Secret Beach is not so secret anymore but the trail is still unmarked.

It is a steady one quarter mile of downhill until a short rock scramble is required to reach the sand. Taking a right will take you to a small waterfall.

Location
42.1918, -124.3670

WALK: Natural Bridges
.2 mi 30' elv :15 EASY

Spectacular rock formations on the Oregon coast.

Natural Bridges can be reached via a .2 mile section of the Oregon Coast trail from the same parking lot as Secret Beach.

Location
42.1918, -124.3670

HIKE: Stout Memorial Grove
.6 mi 32' elv :15 EASY

Stout Memorial grove is a short but must see trail in the redwoods.

A short distance from the trailhead is a split that forms a loop. Taking the trail to the left is the most scenic. At the back of the loop is a spur that will take you down to the river.

Location
41.7898376, -124.0846780

HIKE: Grove of the Titans
1.7 mi 147' elv 1:00 EASY

Another magnificent grove tucked away in a sheltered glen with a small creek running throughout.

Location
41.7725672, -124.0995388

Day 25 *Activities*

HIKE: Boy Scout Tree Loop
3.5 mi 577' elv 2:00 MODERATE

This less touristy trail offers a wilder look at its redwood groves.

The trail crosses several bridges on the way to the Boy Scout Tree. It is possible to continue further to Fern Falls (not to be confused with Fern Canyon) adding another mile and a half to the hike.

Location
41.7686538, -124.1101918

HIKE: Big Trees
2.5 mi 435' elv 1:30 MODERATE

The trail is lined with monster redwoods, lush ferns, lichens and mosses that add a jungle-like appearance to the area.

Take the Big Tree Loop Trail and turn right onto the Cathedral Tree Trail. After crossing Cal Barrel Road the trail descends to an intersection with the Rhododendron Trail and crosses the highway to the visitors center. Take a right onto the Karl Knapp Prarie Creek Trail for 1 mile and take a right onto the Karl Knapp Connector Trail. Cross the highway and take a right on the Foothill Trail to return to the parking area.

Location
41.3731234, -124.013667

Park History: Redwood National Park

Redwood National Park was established in 1968. It was the thirty-third National Park to be designated.

Indigenous communities such as the Yurok, Tolowa, Hupa, and Karukhave were the original inhabitants of the redwood forests of California's North Coast. The first Europeans to visit the land near what is now the park were members of the Cabrillo expedition led by Bartolomé Ferrer In 1543. Prior to Jedediah Smith in 1828, no explorer of European descent is known to have explored the interior of the Northern California coastal region. Discovery of gold along the Trinity River in 1850 brought the Gold Rush to the region of the parks. This displaced the Native American Tribes of the area and led to the logging industry that desired the giant trees found in the region. Trees were cut at an alarming rate and with the advent of the mechanical logging almost all of the old growth forest had been cut.

In the 1920s, the Save the Redwoods League helped create Prairie Creek, Del Norte Coast, and Jedediah Smith Redwoods State Parks to preserve the few remaining old growth forests. After lobbying from the league and the Sierra Club, Congress designated other surrounding areas as Redwood National Park. In 1994, the National Park Service and the California Department of Parks and Recreation combined Redwood National Park with the three abutting Redwoods State Parks into a single administrative unit. In recognition of the rare ecosystem and cultural history found in the park, the United Nations designated it as a World Heritage Site in 1980.

Redwood National Park

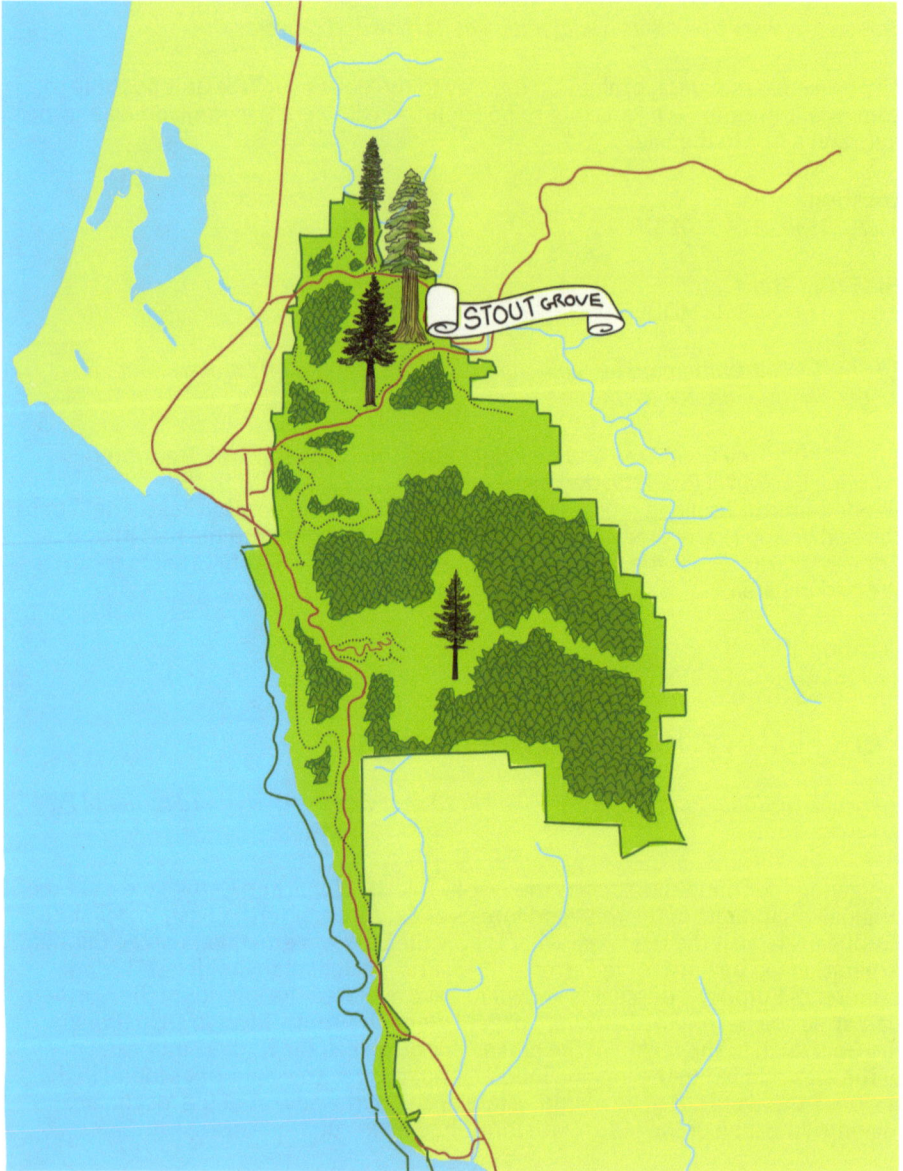

STOUT GROVE

Campground

Gold Bluffs Beach Campground
Davison Rd, Orick, CA 95555
(707) 465-7335
41.382217, -124.069882

Fern Canyon Loop

HIKE: Fern Canyon - Miner's Ridge Clinton Loop
9 mi 790' elv 4:00 MODERATE

Starting from The Gold Bluffs Beach Campground walk the Coastal Trail along the beach for 1.5 miles to reach the parking area for the Fern Canyon Trail. Much of the trail in the canyon is in the stream bed. At the end of the canyon continue onto the James Irvine trail. After another two miles take a right onto the Clintonia Trail. Follow the trail until the intersection with the Miners Ridge trail and take a right to follow the trail west and back to the Campground.

Day 27

Gold Bluffs Beach, CA - Lassen Volcanic National Park, CA

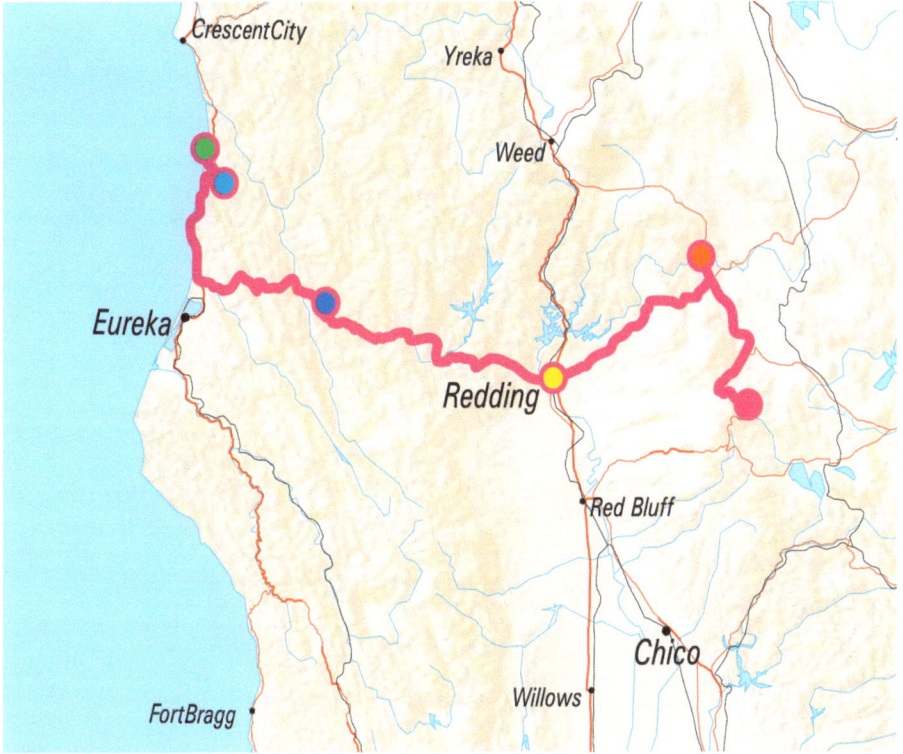

LOCATION	DISTANCE	TIME
Gold Bluffs Beach, CA	0 mi	0:00
Lady Bird Johnson Grove, CA	10 mi	0:30
Gray Falls, CA	97 mi	2:15
RESUPPLY Redding, CA	187 mi	4:15
Burney Falls, CA	250 mi	5:30
Summit Lake South Campground, CA	304 mi	6:30
Total	304 mi	6:30

Campground

Summit Lake South Campground
Mineral, CA 96063
(530) 595-6121
40.4902778, -121.4236111

Bald Eagle

Day 27 *Activities*

HIKE: Lady Bird Johnson Grove
1.4 mi 101' elv :30 EASY

Across the bridge from the parking area is the loop through this higher elevation and more open redwood grove found at the top of a ridge.

Location
41.3033385, -124.0181140

WALK: Grays Falls

A short trail leads out of the back of this campground picnic area to a small creek.

Location
40.85376, -123.48617

HIKE: Burney Falls
1.1 mi 167' :30 EASY

This trail offers close-up views of the spectacular 129' Burney Falls, starting at an overlook and descending to the base of the falls where a large pool can be found. Swimming is no longer permitted.

Location
41.0131796, -121.6505391

HIKE: Summit Lake Loop
.7 mi 22' elv :15 EASY

A short hike around the lake.

Location
Starts at the Summit Lake South campground.

Park History: Lassen Volcanic National Park

Lassen Volcanic National Park was established in 1916. It was the seventeenth National Park designated.

Before European settlers, the Atsugewi, Yana, Yahi, and Maidu tribes would come to the area for hunting and gathering during warmer months, however the climate was not suitable for year round occupation. In 1859 Local Indians were rounded up by militia and taken to Round Valley Indian Reservation. In 1860 Edward R. Drake settled in the Warner Valley. In 1868 The C. Brewster-Clarence King party climbed Lassen Peak.

From May 1914 until 1917, a series of volcanic eruptions occurred on Lassen. Because of the eruptive activity and the area's stark volcanic beauty, Lassen Peak, Cinder Cone, and the area surrounding were established as a National Park.

Lassen Volcanic National Park, CA - Yosemite National Park, CA

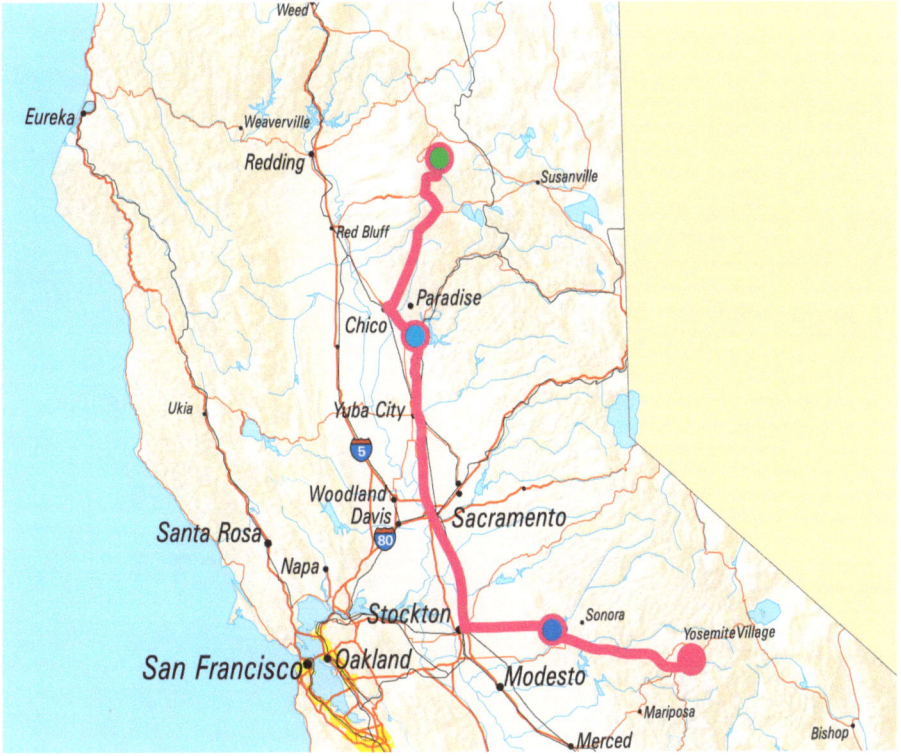

LOCATION	DISTANCE	TIME
🟢 Summit Lake South Campground, CA	0 mi	0:00
🟢 Bumpass Hell, CA	8 mi	0:20
🟢 Sulphur Works, CA	15 mi	0:35
🔵 North Forebay Picnic Area, CA	105 mi	2:30
🔵 Tulloch Lake, CA	270 mi	5:05
🔴 Yosemite Lodge, CA	340 mi	7:10
Total	340 mi	7:10

Lodging

Yosemite Lodge
9006 Yosemite Lodge Dr., CA 95389
(888) 413-8869
37.7435 -119.5983

Clark's Nutcracker

Day 28 *Activities*

HIKE: Bumpass Hell
3 mi 493' elv 1:30 EASY

This is a geothermal area with many steam vents that continuously pour out steam and sulphur gasses from the molten layer running five miles under the surface.

After a short climb over the hillside that obscures this area from the parking lot, the trail begins to descend to a boardwalk that circumnavigates the pools, geysers, and steam vents. Once the boardwalk is completed head back uphill the way you came.

Location
40.4658902, -121.5145644

WALK: Sulphur Works
.3 mi 29' elv :15 EASY

This short walk on a paved path takes one through a hydrothermal area of vibrant colors, sounds, and smells.

Location
40.4486724, -121.5360454

REST: North Forebay Picnic Area

A picnic area to take a break.

Location
39.5356871, -121.5861265

REST: Tulloch Lake

A simple rest stop.

Location
37.8972726, -120.5718653

History: John Muir

John Muir helped inspire the nations connection with the lands that would become our National Parks.

Once a simple shepherd, Muir became the voice for conservation. His writing has inspired generations of American's to get out and enjoy our natural treasures.

"Everybody needs beauty as well as bread, places to play in and pray in, where Nature may heal and cheer and give strength to body and soul alike."

— John Muir

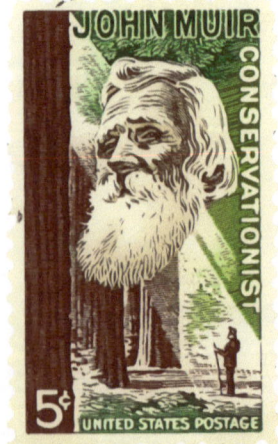

JOHN MUIR CONSERVATIONIST

5¢ UNITED STATES POSTAGE

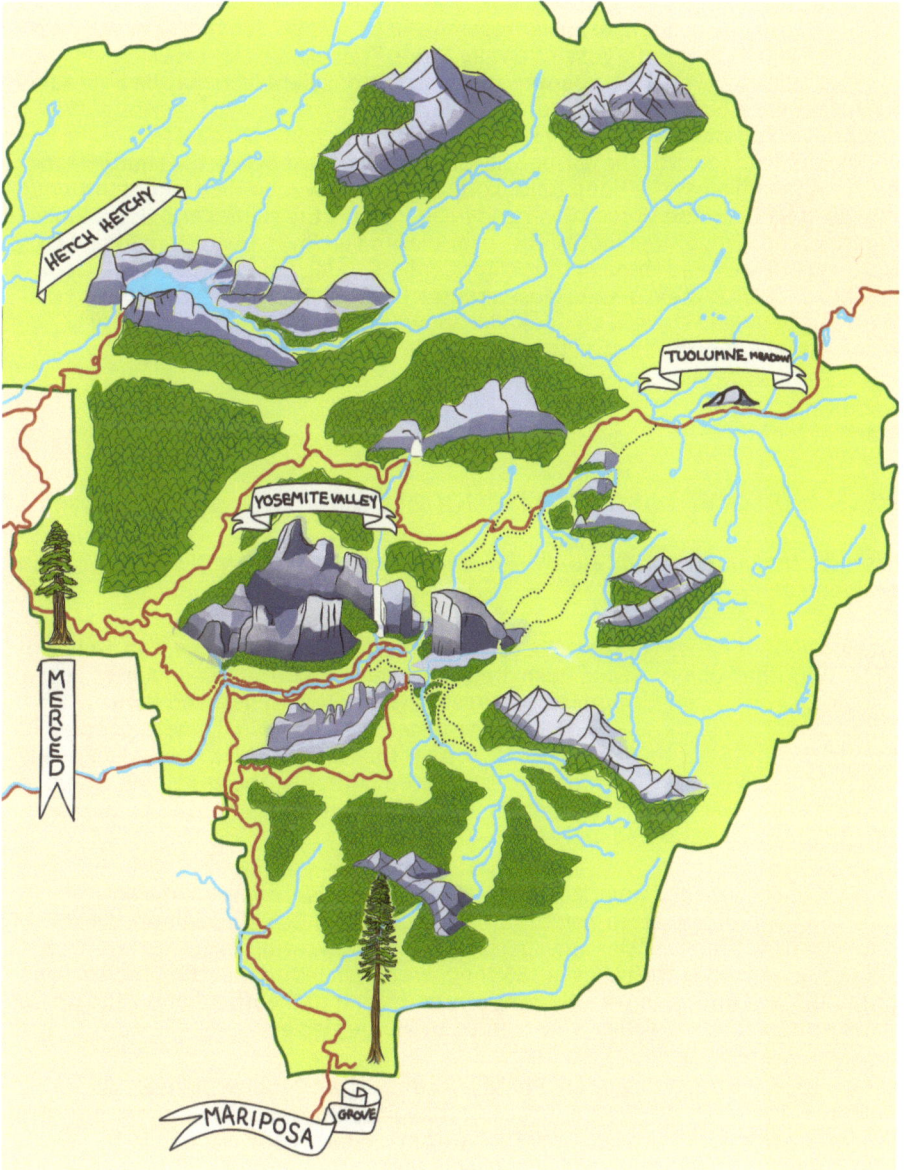

Day 29
Yosemite National Park, CA

Lodging

Yosemite Lodge
9006 Yosemite Lodge Dr., CA 95389
(888) 413-8869
37.7435 -119.5983

Day 29 *Activities*

HIKE: Lower Falls Valley Loop Trail to Mirror Lake
9.6 mi 831' elv 5:00 MODERATE

Begin this loop by heading to Lower Yosemite Falls. This section is on a paved path. Leaving the falls follow the Yosemite Valley Loop Trail towards Mirror Lake. This 2.5 mile section takes you past Yosemite Village to Mirror Lake which may be a meadow by midsummer. From the northwest side of the lake cross Tenaya Creek on a footbridge. Follow the trail on the south side until you reach the east side of the lake. Follow the path towards the Mirror Lake Shuttle Stop. Just before the shuttle stop head south and cross the Happy Isles Loop Road. Follow the Valley Footpath along the north banks of the Merced River and head towards the stables and North Pines Campground. Cross three footbridges over the Merced River. Head straight and cross Northside Drive. Head through the Visitor Center Parking Lot to the Sidewalk Trail and head towards the Yosemite Museum. Head west on the Valley Paved Path, cross Oak Lane and head straight on Cook's Meadow Loop. Take a right onto Lower Yosemite Falls Loop and return to the Yosemite Lodge.

Location
Starts at the Yosemite Lodge.

Park History: Yosemite National Park

Yosemite National Park was established in 1890. It was the third National Park to be designated.

The indigenous natives of Yosemite called themselves the Ahwahneechee. Between 1848-1855, the California Gold Rush drew more than 90,000 European Americans to the area, causing competition for resources between gold miners and Native Americans. The Mariposa War ordered the systemic killing of indigenous peoples throughout the State between 1840-1870. After the Mariposa War, Native Americans continued to live in the Yosemite area in reduced numbers. The remaining Yosemite Ahwahneechee were forced to relocate to a village constructed in 1851 by the state. By 1953, no natives resided in the park.

In 1855, entrepreneur James Mason Hutchingsand artist Thomas Ayres were amongst the first tourists to visit the area and created much of Yosemite's early publicity by writhing articles and special editions showcasing its natural wonders. John Muir arrived to the valley in 1868 and wrote articles popularizing the area and promoting scientific interest. Muir was one of the first to theorize that the major landforms in Yosemite Valley were created by alpine glaciers.

In May 1903, President Theodore Roosevelt camped with John Muir near Glacier Point for three days. While camping, Muir convinced Roosevelt to take the control of Yosemite Valley and Mariposa Grove away from California and return it to the federal government. In 1906, Roosevelt signed a bill that shifted control.

In 1916, the National Park Service granted a 20-year concession to the Desmond Park Service Company which built hotels and other facilities in the valley. The two merged into the Yosemite Park & Curry Company and built the Ahwahnee Hotel in 1926–27.

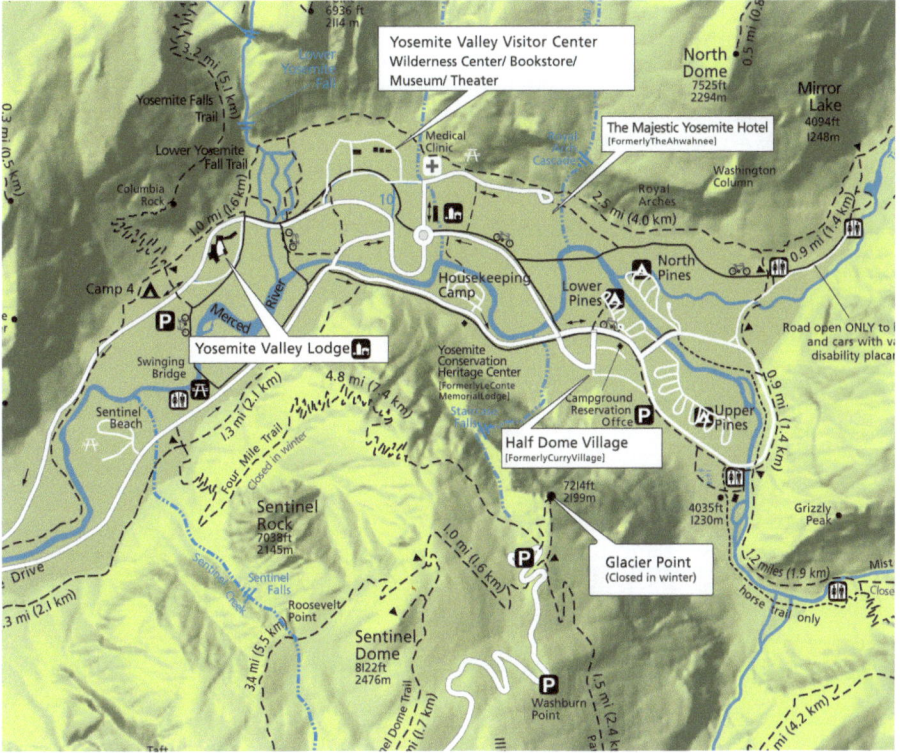

"It is by far the grandest of all the special temples of Nature I was ever permitted to enter."

— John Muir

Lodging

Lower Pines Campground
9000 Southside Dr, TUOLUMNE MEADOWS
(209) 372-8502
37.7407699, -119.5673036

Black Bear

Day 30 *Activities*

HIKE: Sentinel Dome Trail
5.2 mi 1222' elv 3:30 MODERATE

The best views are found beyond the end of the Glacier Point Road.

Sentinel Dome offers 360-degree panoramic views of Yosemite Valley from a dome that begins 2 miles before the end of the Glacier Point Road. The wide trail follows along mostly exposed granite without much shade. Past Sentinel Dome is a loop that heads west then south and crossing Sentinel Creek on the Pohono Trail. Take a right at a junction to continue on the Pohono Trail to Taft Point. From Taft Point return the way you came in and take a right at the junction to return to the parking area. This is not the place to be during a thunderstorm.

Location
37.7124626, -119.5863640

Park History: Best's Studio (Ansel Adams Gallery)

Best's Studio now hosts a collection of Ansel Adams and other contemporary works.

Best's Studio was one of several artists' studios operating in Yosemite Valley at the turn of the twentieth century. A young Ansel Adams often played the piano at Best's Studio. Ansel met his wife Virginia there and it is where he first publicly exhibited his art. He and his family lived and worked at the studio through the late 1940s.

Parkitecture: Ahwahnee Hotel

A blend of stone and wood that was built to match the surrounding of the valley.

Known for its stunning interior design and architecture, The Ahwahnee was designed to highlight its natural surroundings that include Yosemite Falls, Half Dome, and Glacier Point.

Commissioned in the 1920s to draw affluent visitors to Yosemite National Park, The Ahwahnee is a testament to American ingenuity. More than 5,000 tons of stone, 1,000 tons of steel, and 30,000 feet of lumber were transported through the mountains to create the hotel. The hotel was completed in 1927.

The Ahwahnee has been visited by presidents, royalty and celebrities.

YOSEMITE

NATIONAL

PARK

Hetch Hetchy
Reservoir

Tuolumne River

Tuolumne River

Highway 120
closed in winter

120

To
Lee Vinin

Hetch
Hetchy

White Wolf
(open seasonally)

Tioga Road closed
November to May
west of this point

Tioga Road

Mather

Facilities along
Tioga Road available
summer only

Porcupine Flat
(open seasonally)

Tuolumne
Meadows
(open seasonally)

To
San
Francisco
120

Tioga Road closed
November to May
east of this point

Hodgdon
Meadow

Yosemite Creek
(open seasonally)

Tenaya
Lake

Tamarack Flat
(open seasonally)

Yosemite Valley

Crane Flat
(open seasonally)

YOSEMITE VALLEY

Glacier
Point

Merced River

El
Portal

Glacier Point Road
closed November to
May east of this point

Glacier Point Road

Merced River

140

Bridalveil Creek
(open seasonally)

To
Merced

Paved road

Unpaved road

Campground

Wawona

South Fork Merced River

North

0   5 Kilometers

0   5 Miles

Mariposa Grove

41

To Fresno   Fish Camp

Lodging

Lower Pines Campground
9000 Southside Dr, TUOLUMNE MEADOWS
(209) 372-8502
37.7407699, -119.5673036

Mist Trail

HIKE: Mist Trail
7.3 mi 2,600' elv 5:30 HARD

This impressively crafted trail brings the hiker to the spectacular Vernal and Nevada Falls. The trail begins at the Happy Isles shuttle stop on a paved and scenic trail that crosses the Merced River to ascend through the mist of the 317' Vernal Falls on a series of 600 granite steps. From the top of the falls, continue to the top of the massive 594' Nevada Falls. From here you can either return the way you came or follow a loop back on the John Muir Trail.

LOCATION	DISTANCE	TIME
🟢 Lower Pines Campground, CA	0 mi	0:00
🔵 Sunrise Lakes Trailhead, CA	48 mi	1:20
🔵 Buckeye Hot Springs, CA	112 mi	3:00
🔴 Big Pine Creek Campground, CA	237 mi	5:30
Total	237 mi	5:30

Campground

Big Pine Creek Campground
Inyo,CA
(760) 935-4339
37.1258333, -118.4325

Pika

Day 32 *Activities*

HIKE: Tenaya Creek Waterslide
3 mi 150' elv 2:00 MODERATE

The Tenaya Creek Waterslide is a 100' long smooth granite waterslide that dumps into a 3' deep swimming hole.

The hike is mostly off-trail but if you follow the creek you will find it. Start at the Sunrise trailhead and follow the dirt trail until it crosses Tenaya Creek. Leave the trail and follow the eastern side of the creek, often along slabs of granite, until the top of the slid is reached. Carefully descend the slide to the pool below.

Location
37.8256706, -119.4703561

SOAK: Buckeye Hot Springs

Situated on the edge of a creek, the geothermal source cascades down a ledge into a rock lined pool where the hot waterfall and cold creek water mix to form the perfect soaking pool.

The pools can be reached from the road above via a short but steep path. Part way down the hill is a secondary pool that is perfect if the lower pool is submerged in high water. An alternate approach can be made from Buckeye Campground which is just a quarter mile upstream.

Location
38.2398281, -119.3258079

Buckeye Hot Springs

Campground

Big Pine Creek Campground
Inyo,CA
(760) 935-4339
37.1258333, -118.4325

Day 33 *Activities*

HIKE: Big Pine Lakes
9.7 mi 2,945' elv 7:00 HARD

Big pine Lakes is one of the jewels of the Sierra that does not require an extremely lengthy approach.

This hike is not easy, in-fact it is the hardest hike on this trip, but by now you should be in shape enough to enjoy it. Following the North Fork of Big Pine Creek, the trail traverses 2 miles of shadeless hillside until passing above a waterfall and entering forest. Soon you will reach Lon Chaney's Cabin which marks the mid point of the hike and has shaded spots nestled by the creek perfect for a break. The next 3 miles follows a series of switchbacks and the incline is moderate but steady until you reach the first lake. It is only a short distance further to second lake where excellent lunch spots can be found. It is possible to visit 5 other lake that increase in elevation another 2,000' and add 4 more miles to the hike.

Location
Starts from the Big Pine Creek Campground.

Tips: Heat Stroke

The next leg of the journey brings you to the desert. Drink lots of fluids, use electrolytes and protect your body, head, and eyes from the sun.

SYMPTOMS

High Body Temperature

Nausea

Headache

Rapid Pulse

Unconciousness

Flushed dry skin

Dizzyness

Thirst

Dry Swollen Tongue

No Sweat

If you experience any of these symptoms get out of the sun immediately.

FIRST AID

Move Out of Sun

Drink Water

Apply Ice (Neck, Armits)

Run a Fan

Mist With Water

Day 34

Big Pine, CA - Joshua Tree National Park, CA

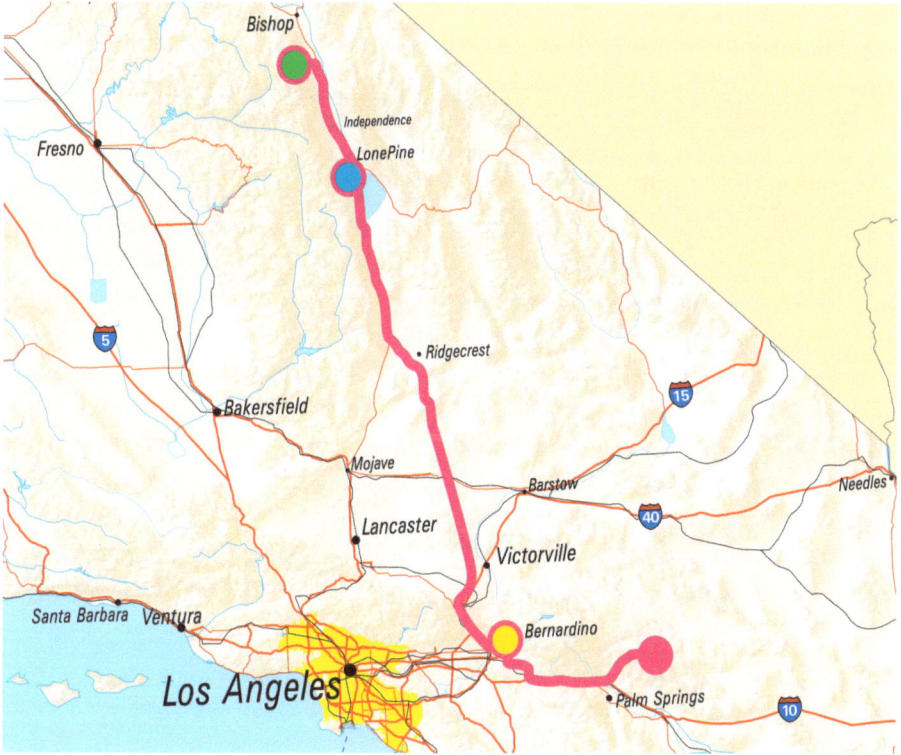

LOCATION	DISTANCE	TIME
🟢 Big Pine Creek Campground, CA	0 mi	0:00
🔵 Mobius Arch, CA	56 mi	1:10
🟡 RESUPPLY Trader Joe's Redlands, CA	260 mi	4:40
🔴 Indian Cove Campground, CA	337 mi	6:00
Total	337 mi	6:00

Campground

Indian Cove Campground
7295 Indian Cove, Twentynine palms, CA 92277
(760) 362-4367
34.12, -116.1558333

Coyote

Day 34 *Activities*

WALK: Mobius Arch

An easy 5 minute drive from the freeway on a dirt road, then a 10 minute walk to an arch that perfectly frames Mount Whitney offers the perfect place to take a break.

The Alabama Hills are a popular filming location for television and movie productions. Among the television shows that have been shot here are The Gene Autry Show, The Lone Ranger, Bonanza, and Annie Oakley. Some of the movies that have been filmed here include, How the West Was Won, Joe Kidd, Saboteur, and Django Unchained.

Location
36.6112220, -118.1250446

RESUPPLY: Trader Joe's

Location
552 Orange St, Redlands, CA 92374
34.0605624, -117.1816921

Park History: Joshua Tree National Park

Joshua Tree National Park was established in 1994. It was the fifty-fourth National Park designated.

Original inhabitants included the Serrano, the Cahuilla, and the Chemehuevi peoples. They occupied the Oasis of Mara in what is now called Twentynine Palms.

By the late 1920s the development of new roads into the desert brought an influx of land developers and cactus poachers. Minerva Hoyt, became concerned about the removal of cacti and other plants for use in the gardens of Los Angeles. Her efforts to protect this area resulted in 825,000 acres being set aside as Joshua Tree National Monument in 1936. It was not until 1994 that it became a National Park.

Tips: Poison Oak

Poison oak and sumac are shrubs. Poison ivy usually grows as a vine on tree trunks or straggling over the ground. They can all cause allergic reactions that itch like crazy.

What to do?

Remove any clothing that has touched the plant. Gently wash skin and scrub under fingernails right away with water and mild soap or dish soap. For itching: Add oatmeal to the bath and put calamine lotion on the skin (but not on the face or on the genitals).

Day 35

Joshua Tree National Park, CA - Grand Canyon , AZ

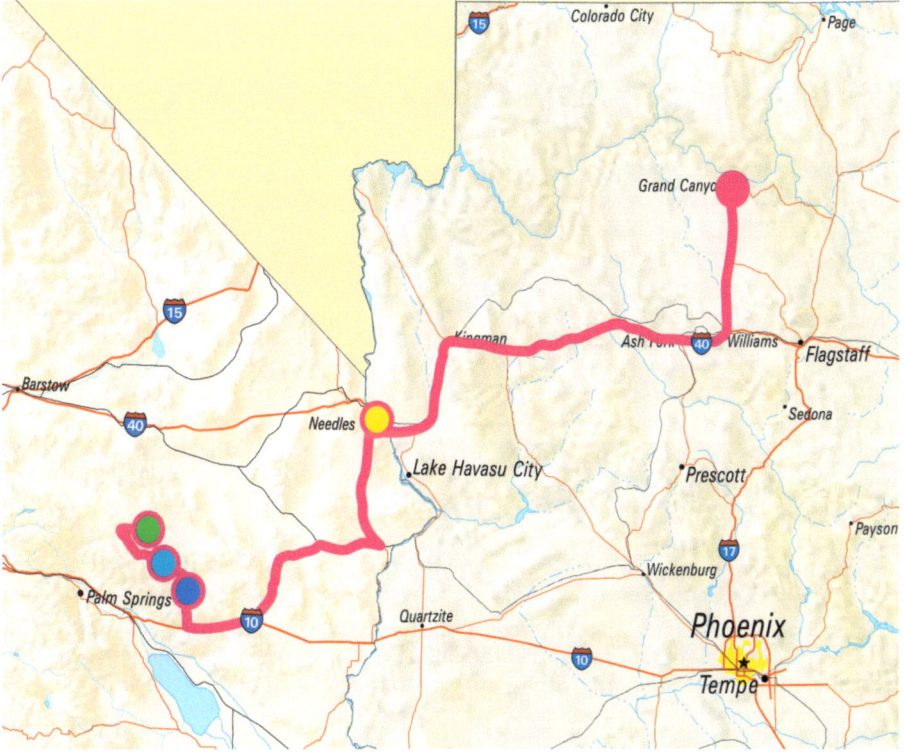

LOCATION	DISTANCE	TIME
🟢 Indian Cove, CA	0 mi	0:00
🔵 Hidden Valley Nature Trail, CA	26 mi	0:40
🔵 Skull Rock Nature Trail, CA	34mi	0:55
🔵 Arch Rock, CA	39 mi	1:05
🔵 Cottonwood Springs Lost Palm Oasis, CA	69 mi	1:45
🟡 Colorado River Beach, CA	220 mi	3:15
🔴 Bright Angel Lodge, AZ	424 mi	7:00
Total	424 mi	7:00

Campground

Bright Angel Lodge
9 Village Loop Drive, Grand Canyon, AZ 86023
(928) 638-2631
36.05743, -112.14284

Woodpecker

Day 35 *Activities*

HIKE: Hidden Valley
1 mi 118' elv :30 EASY

An easy scenic hike through a valley surrounded by rock formations.

Location
34.0123314, -116.1679966

HIKE: Skull Rock
1.7 mi 147' elv :40 EASY

An easy hike amongst Joshua Tree's signature rock formations.

Skull Rock is immediately across from the parking area but a larger loop trail exists that also visits Jumbo Rocks as it meanders through the campground.

Location
33.9978738, -116.0598835

HIKE: Arch Rock Trail
1.9 mi 88' elv 1:00 EASY

An easy hike to a natural arch.

This trail begins at a parking lot labeled Twin Tanks. Walk to the south end of the parking lot parallel to the road and within 250' the trail crosses the road to the east side and continues to the arch. Along the way to the left of the trail is Heart Rock.

Location
33.9900271, -116.0228063

HIKE: Cottonwood Spring
.1 mi 7' elv :15 MODERATE

A short walk into an oasis in the desert.

Location
33.7369770, -115.8106570

SWIM: Colorado River Beach

Take a break and get in the Colorado River.

An unmarked pullout leads to a short hike east along Moabi inlet to a small beach on the Colorado River.

Location
34.72694, -114.49973

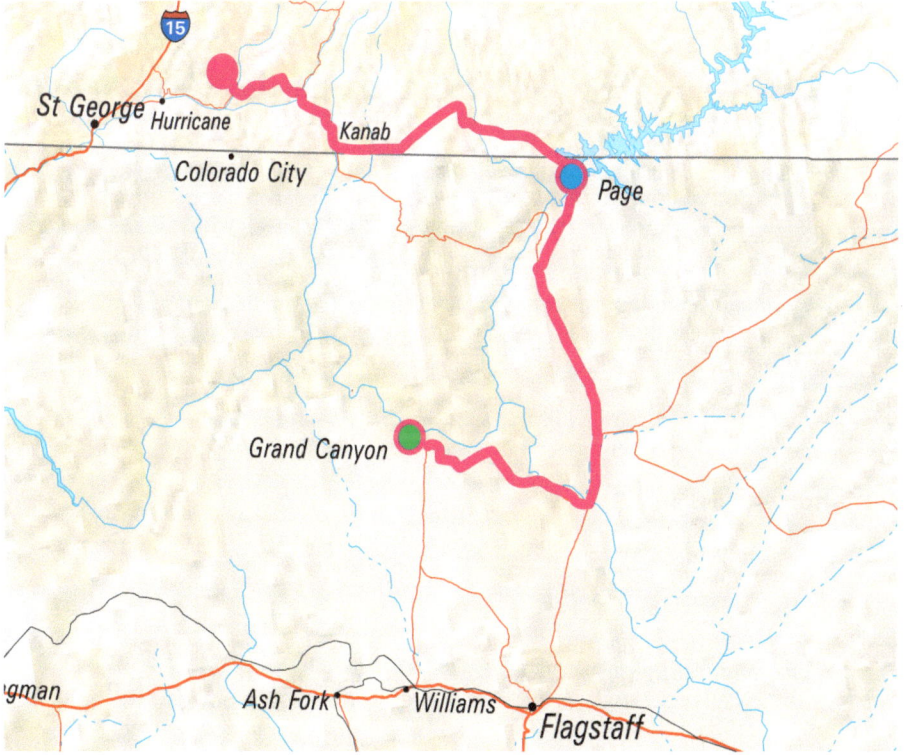

LOCATION	DISTANCE	TIME
🟢 Grand Canyon, AZ	0 mi	0:00
🔵 Horseshoe Bend, AZ	135 mi	2:30
🔴 Zion Lodge, UT	265 mi	4:50
Total	265 mi	4:50

Lodging

Zion Park Lodge
1 Zion Lodge Springdale, UT 84767
(435) 772-7700
37.2502 N, -112.9564

Golden Mantle Squirrel

Day 36 *Activities*

HIKE: South Rim Trail from Bright Angel to Hermits Rest
7.7 mi 1243' elv 4:00 MODERATE

A Moderate hike along the south rim. Go as far as you like and take a shuttle back..

Get on the Rim Trail and head west towards Trailhead Overlook. Next head towards Maricopa Point. From here the path heads away from the rim for a stretch between Maricopa and Powell Points. After Powell Point the trail continues along the side of the road to Hopi Point. Hopi Point is one of the most popular places to view the sunset. From Hopi Point hop back on the paved Rim Trail which soon turns to dirt. Soon you will arrive at Mojave Point. Continue on the trail as it winds its way on and off the road. The trail heads away from the edge for a while until it reaches the Monument Creek vista. Monument Creek Vista marks the start of the Hermit Road Greenway Trail, a section of the Rim Trail that's paved and takes you to Pima Point. Past Pima point the trail takes you to Hermit's Rest where you can visit the Hermit's Rest building from 1914 that is built in the "National Park Rustic" style.

Location
Starts from the Bright Angel Lodge.

HIKE: Horseshoe Bend
1.5 mi 137' elv :45 EASY

One of the most iconic views in the American Southwest.

Horseshoe Bend, just 9 miles upstream from the Grand Canyon, has become one of the most iconic spots in the American Southwest. It's a short hike but worth every second. The Park is open from Sunrise to Sunset and has bathrooms at the trailhead. A $10 entrance fee is charged.

Location
36.8763848, -111.50152

HIKE: Emerald Pools and Grotto Trail
3.2 mi 620' elv 1:30 MODERATE

The Emerald Pools is a unique desert oasis that features three distinct pools. The waterfalls that feed into these pools do not flow year round so the best time to visit is in the spring or after a period of rain.

From the Zion Lodge (Shuttle Stop 5), walk across Zion Canyon Road to reach the Emerald Pools Trailhead. Take the bridge across the Virgin River. Start with the Lower Emerald Pools Trail first which will soon take you behind the first waterfall. After the Lower Pool the trail takes you up 400' to reach the Upper Pool. A split in the trail will take you to the right to an overlook of the Lower Pool. Take a left to continue to the Middle and Upper Pools. Returning to the Lower Emerald Pools Trial take a left onto the Kayenta Trail and follow it north to a bridge over the Virgin River. Walk through the Grotto Oicnic area and take a right on the Grotto Trail to return to the Zion Lodge.

Location
Starts from the Zion Lodge.

Lodging

Zion Park Lodge
1 Zion Lodge Springdale, UT 84767
(435) 772-7700
37.2502 N, -112.9564

The Narrows

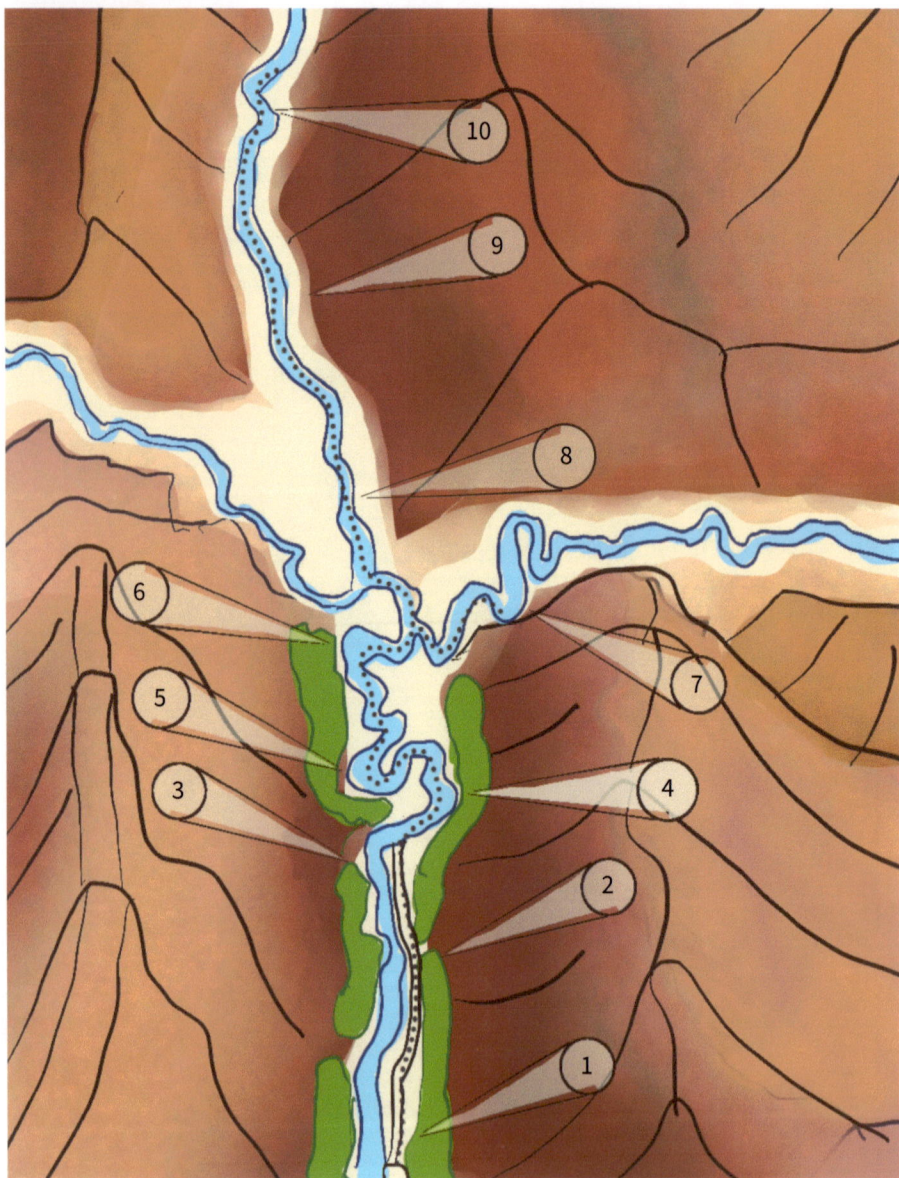

FEATURES

1. Temple of Sinawava
2. Riverside Walk
3. End of paved trail
4. Mystery Canyon Falls
5. House Rock
6. Narrows Alcove
7. Veiled Falls
8. Floating Rock
9. End of Wall Street
10. Big Springs TURN AROUND

Day 37 *Activities*

HIKE: The Narrows Bottom Up
9.4 mi 695' elv 8:00 HARD

This is a unique adventure that involves wading a river beneath towering cliffs.

From the Lodge get on the Shuttle at stop #5 - Shuttle Stop #9 Temple of Sinawava.

Make sure to check conditions with the ranger station before setting out to ensure that there is no flash flood expected. If the probability monitor reads "probable" start hiking out as soon as there is a sign of rain.

River is ideal when < 70 CFS (expect to get wet from the waist down)

Feature	Distance	Time
Temple of Sinawava Shuttle Stop	0.0	0
End of paved Riverside Walk	1.0	0:20
Mystery Falls	1.3	0:35
House Rock	1.7	1:00
Narrows Alcove	2.0	1:45
Orderville Canyon / Wall Street	3.0	2:00
Floating Rock	3.7	2:30
End of Wall Street	4.2	3:00
Big Springs	4.7	4:20

End of paved Riverside Walk
From here out you are walking in the river.

Mystery Canyon Falls
A 110' falls that descends from the canyon walls above.

House Rock
The presence of this rock narrows the river to 10' wide.

Narrows Alcove
The walls of the canyon overhang this bend in the river.

Orderville Canyon / Wall Street
Orderville Canyon is on the right, the only spur in the canyon, and offers a small 1/4 mile section away from the crowds that can be explored without a permit.

Floating Rock
A huge boulder that bisects the riverbed. Near Floating Rock is a small raised bank that is a perfect rest spot out of the water.

End of Wall Street
The canyon walls widen here and a series of boulder scrambles bring you to Sipping Turtle a feature that can be heard gurgling like a turtle.

Big Spring
A rushing spring that comes out of the canyon walls. Day hikers must turn around.

Day 37 *Activities*

The Narrows

The hike begins on Riverside Walk, an easy trail that runs beside the Virgin River. The first mile is on dry land, but after that first mile it's time to get wet. The water will be cold but in late July and August it will not be necessary to wear specialized gear. For the next few miles you will be hiking in knee to waist deep water. The terrain on the river floor ranges from sand to slippery rocks.

You will be traveling upstream against the current so hiking poles are useful. Mystery Falls, a 110' waterfall is at 1.5 miles. At 3 miles a tributary leads off to Orderville Canyon on the right. You can explore Orderville canyon for about .5 miles to a small waterfall at which point you must return.

Beyond Ordeville Canyon, this section of the narrows is known as Wall Street. In some places the canyon walls tower up to 2,000' feet above you. This is the most scenic section of the canyon. Most people turn around at about the 3 mile mark for a round trip hike of 6 miles. At 3.7 miles is Floating Rock which bisects the river, and just beyond is an elevated bank that is the perfect place to get out of the water and have lunch. It is possible to continue for another mile to Big Springs which is the northern limit of the hike without requiring a permit and makes for a 9.4 mile round trip.

Park History: Zion National Park

Zion National Park was established in 1919. It was the fifteenth National Park to be designated.

The Zion area was inhabited by the Anasazi from approximately 1,500 to 800 years ago, leaving behind abandoned cliff houses and rock art. When Nephi Johnson arrived in what would become Zion National Park in 1858, the canyon was occupied by the Paiute Indians.

The floor of Zion Canyon was settled in 1863 by Isaac Behunin, who farmed corn, tobacco, and fruit trees. The Behunin family lived in Zion Canyon near the site of today's Zion Lodge during the summer, and wintered in Springdale. They named the area Zion, a reference to the place of peace mentioned in The Bible.

Zion Canyon was accessible by car in the summer of 1917 and Wylie Camp, was set up for tent camping. After establishment as a national park most visitors concentrated in the Zion Canyon until formal trails were built such as Angels Landing and the Narrows River Walk in 1926. The CCC completed the many remaining trails in the 1930s.

Work on the Zion – Mount Carmel Highway started in 1927 and completed in 1930. The most famous feature of the Zion – Mount Carmel Highway is its 1.1-mile tunnel, which has six large windows cut through the massive sandstone cliff.

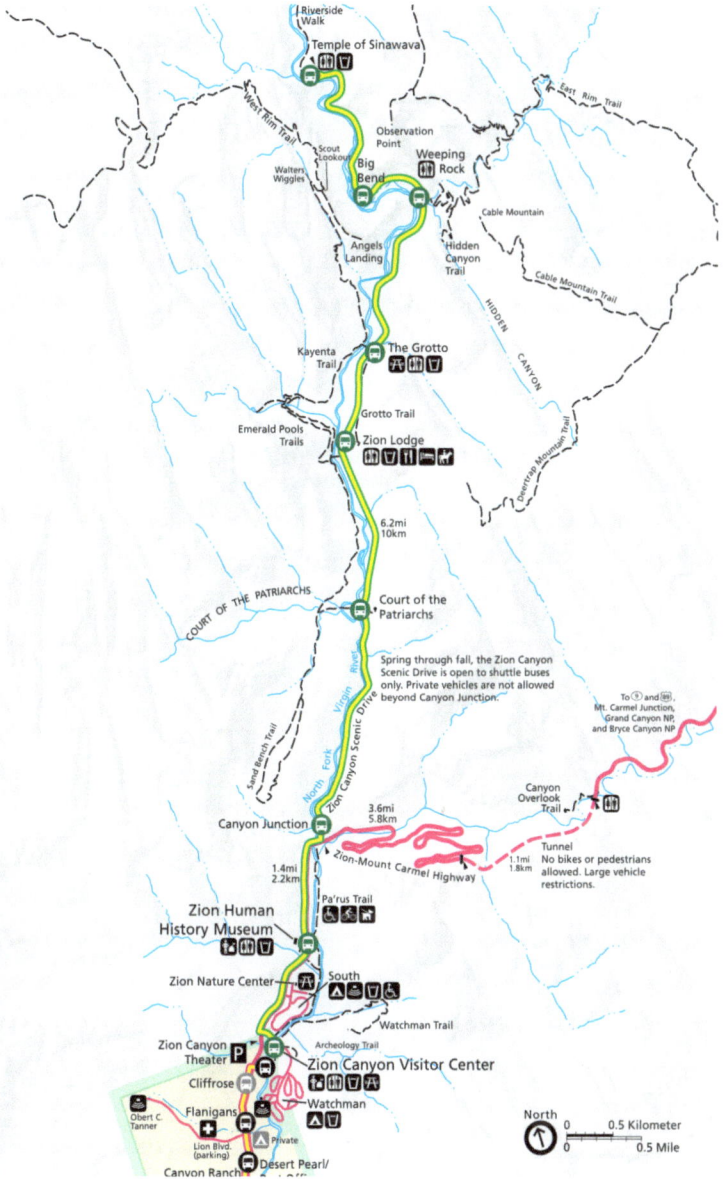

Riverside
Walk
Temple of Sinawava

East Rim Trail

West Rim Trail

Observation
Point
Scout
Lookout
Walters
Wiggles
Big
Bend
Weeping
Rock

Cable Mountain

Angels
Landing
Hidden
Canyon
Trail

Cable Mountain Trail

HIDDEN CANYON

Kayenta
Trail
The Grotto

Grotto Trail

Deertrap Mountain Trail

Emerald Pools
Trails
Zion Lodge

6.2mi
10km

COURT OF THE PATRIARCHS

Court of the
Patriarchs

Virgin River

Spring through fall, the Zion Canyon
Scenic Drive is open to shuttle buses
only. Private vehicles are not allowed
beyond Canyon Junction.

To and
Mt. Carmel Junction,
Grand Canyon NP
and Bryce Canyon NP

Sand Bench Trail

North Fork

Zion Canyon Scenic Drive

Canyon
Overlook
Trail

Canyon Junction

3.6mi
5.8km

Zion-Mount Carmel Highway

1.1mi
1.8km
Tunnel
No bikes or pedestrians
allowed. Large vehicle
restrictions.

1.4mi
2.2km

Pa'rus Trail

Zion Human
History Museum

Zion Nature Center

South

Watchman Trail

Zion Canyon
Theater

Archeology Trail

Zion Canyon Visitor Center

Cliffrose

Watchman

Obert C.
Tanner

Flanigans

North
0   0.5 Kilometer
0   0.5 Mile

Lion Blvd.
(parking)

Private

Desert Pearl/
Canyon Ranch

Campground

Watchman Campground
1 Zion Park Blvd. Springdale, UT 84767
(435) 772-3256
37.1964, -112.9876

Day 38 *Activities*

HIKE: Scout Lookout via West Rim Trail
3.6 mi 1122' elv 3:00 HARD

Scouts lookout follows much of the same trail as Angel's Landing without the chains section at the very top.

The trail begins from the Grotto shuttle stop which can also be reached on foot from the Zion Lodge.

First cross the bridge over the Virgin River and head upstream on the West Rim Trail. Then climb the lower slopes before beginning a set of switchbacks on the cliff wall. There is a break from the climbing and the sun as you hike through Refrigerator Canyon before ascending the tight switchbacks called Walter's Wiggles to Scout Lookout. A bathroom can be found near Scouts Lookout.

Location
Starts from the Grotto Shuttle Stop.

DRIVE: Zion Lodge -Watchman Campground
5 mi :10

Parkitecture: Zion Lodge

A blend of stone and wood that was built to match the surrounding of the valley.

With the completion of a Union Pacific Railroad spur line to nearby Cedar City, Utah in 1923, visitors now had an easy and comfortable way to get to Zion. The Utah Parks Company, a subsidiary of the Union Pacific Railroad took on the challenge of building accommodations that would be suitable for the influx of visitors to the park. Gilbert Stanley Underwood, whom architected numerous national park lodges, designed the main lodge. The Zion Lodge was completed in May of 1925. Later a series of stand-alone cabins were built nearby.

The main lodge building stood for over forty years until it was consumed by a fire on January 26, 1966. A mere 108 days after the fire, a new building was up and operating in its place.

Tips: Poison Ivy

Poison ivy usually grows as a vine on tree trunks or straggling over the ground; poison oak and sumac are shrubs. They can all cause allergic reactions that itch like crazy.

What to do?

Remove any clothing that has touched the plant. Gently wash skin and scrub under fingernails right away with water and mild soap or dish soap. For itching: Add oatmeal to the bath and put calamine lotion on the skin (but not on the face or on the genitals).

Day 39

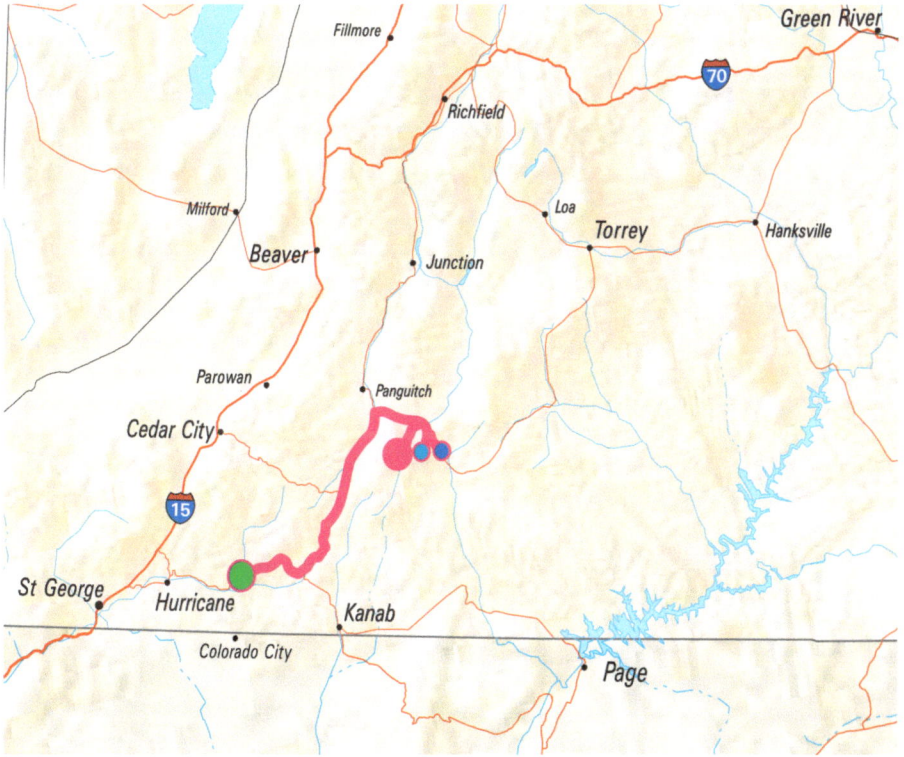

LOCATION	DISTANCE	TIME
🟢 Zion National Park, UT	0 mi	0:00
🟢 Zion Canyon Overlook, UT	7 mi	0:15
🔵 Mossy Cave Trailhead, UT	84 mi	1:25
🔵 RESUPPLY: Tropic, UT	87 mi	1:35
🔴 North Campground, UT	95 mi	1:45
Total	95 mi	1:45

Campground

North Campground
Bryce Canyon City, UT 84764
(435) 834-5322
37.6344444, -112.1669444

Long Tailed Weasel

111

Day 39 *Activities*

HIKE: Mossy Cave Trail
1 mi 121' :30 EASY

There are two great payoffs along this trail: A waterfall, and Mossy Cave.

This is a short hike that follows a stream most of the way. There is a bridge that overlooks the falls from about 100 yards away, but there is a user trail to the base of the falls that affords a more intimate view. At the fork, the right takes you to the top of the falls and the left takes you around to the grotto called Mossy Cave. The grotto area is cool and shady providing a great place to relax.

Location
UT-12, Tropic, UT 84776
37.665747, -112.110227

HIKE: Navajo Loop and Queens Garden
4.0 mi 777' 2:00 MODERATE

This hike combines Queens Garden with the Navajo Loop Trail and a portion of the Rim Trail, for the overall best hiking experience in Bryce Canyon.

From North Campground head south on the Rim Trail to Sunrise Point and take a left to follow the Queens Garden trail east then south past Queen Victoria until the intersection with the Navajo Loop trail. Follow to Sunset Point and take the Rim Trail back to where you started.

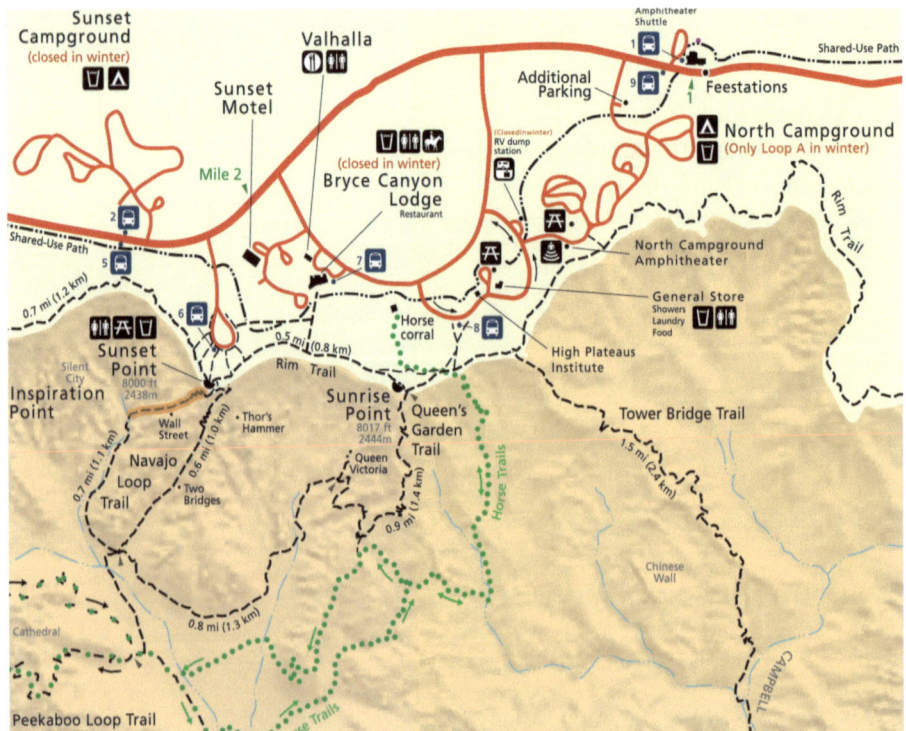

Day 40

LOCATION	DISTANCE	TIME
Bryce Canyon, UT	0 mi	0:00
Lower Calf Creek Falls, UT	70 mi	1:30
Park Avenue, UT	270 mi	5:10
Windows Loop, UT	278 mi	5:25
Devil's Garden Campground, UT	289 mi	5:45
Total	289 mi	5:45

Campground

Devil's Garden Campground
2282 S. West Resources Blvd, Moab, UT 84532-0907
(435) 719-2299
38.7769444, -109.5891667

Kangaroo Rat

Park History: Bryce Canyon National Park

Bryce Canyon National Park was established in 1928. It was the sixteenth National Park to be designated.

In 1916, J.W. Humphrey secured a grant to improve the road and make the rim accessible to automobile traffic. In 1920 the Ruby and Minnie Syrett constructed Tourist's Rest a 30 by 71 foot lodge, that was later acquired by the Union Pacific Railroad. Bryce was designated a National Park in 1928.

Day 40 *Activities*

HIKE: Lower Calf Creek Falls
6.1 mi 531' elv 3:00 MODERATE

The 125' waterfall that plunges into a sand beach lined pool within the canyon is the climax of this journey complete with ancient ruins and rock art from the Native Americans.

Advisory: The hike gets full sun during much of the day with intermittent spots to rest in the shade. This is NOT a hike to do mid-day during summer.

From the parking area, follow the campground road a few hundred yards to the main trail on the left before the campground to cross Calf Creek. The trail climbs a short bit, then levels out as it meanders up the canyon bottom. About 1.25 miles from the parking is interpretative marker 5. This is one not to miss! Across the canyon, on the east side, are several granaries. At about 1.8 miles across the canyon, near the base of the cliff, are 3 red pictograph figures. At 3 miles reach the waterfall and pool.

Location
Mile marker 75 Route 12, Boulder, UT 84716
37.793186, -111.413820

HIKE: Park Avenue
1.8 mi 308' elv :50 EASY

This trail takes you through a canyon lined with towering sandstone walls and spires.

The trail makes its way down the valley between towering walls. About half way down, a side canyon comes in on the left. This makes a nice, short side trip to get away from the crowds. Near the bottom of the hike, Courthouse Towers come into view right before another trailhead is reached. Return the way you came in.

Location
38.6243144, -109.5998665

Lower Calf Creek Falls

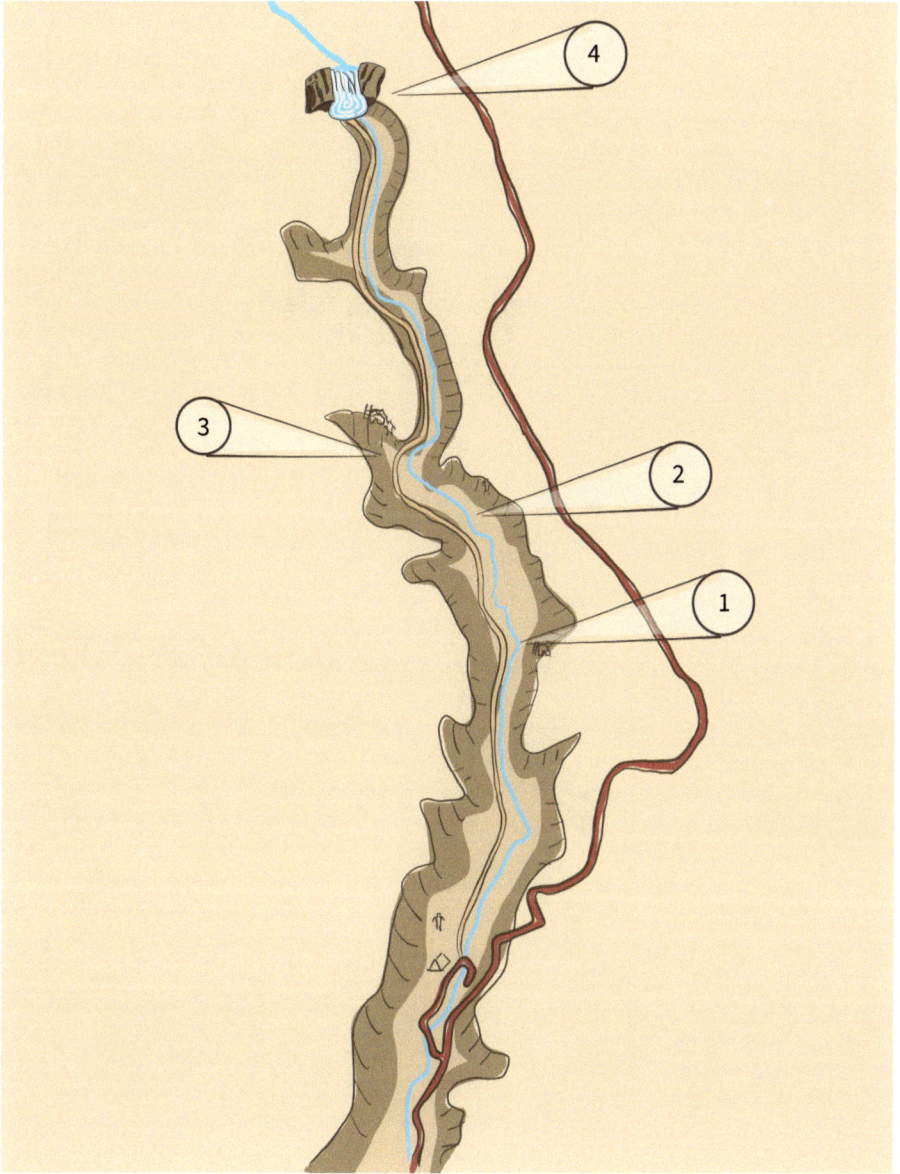

FEATURE

1. Granary view
2. Rock art view
3. Granary view
4. Lower Calf Creek Falls

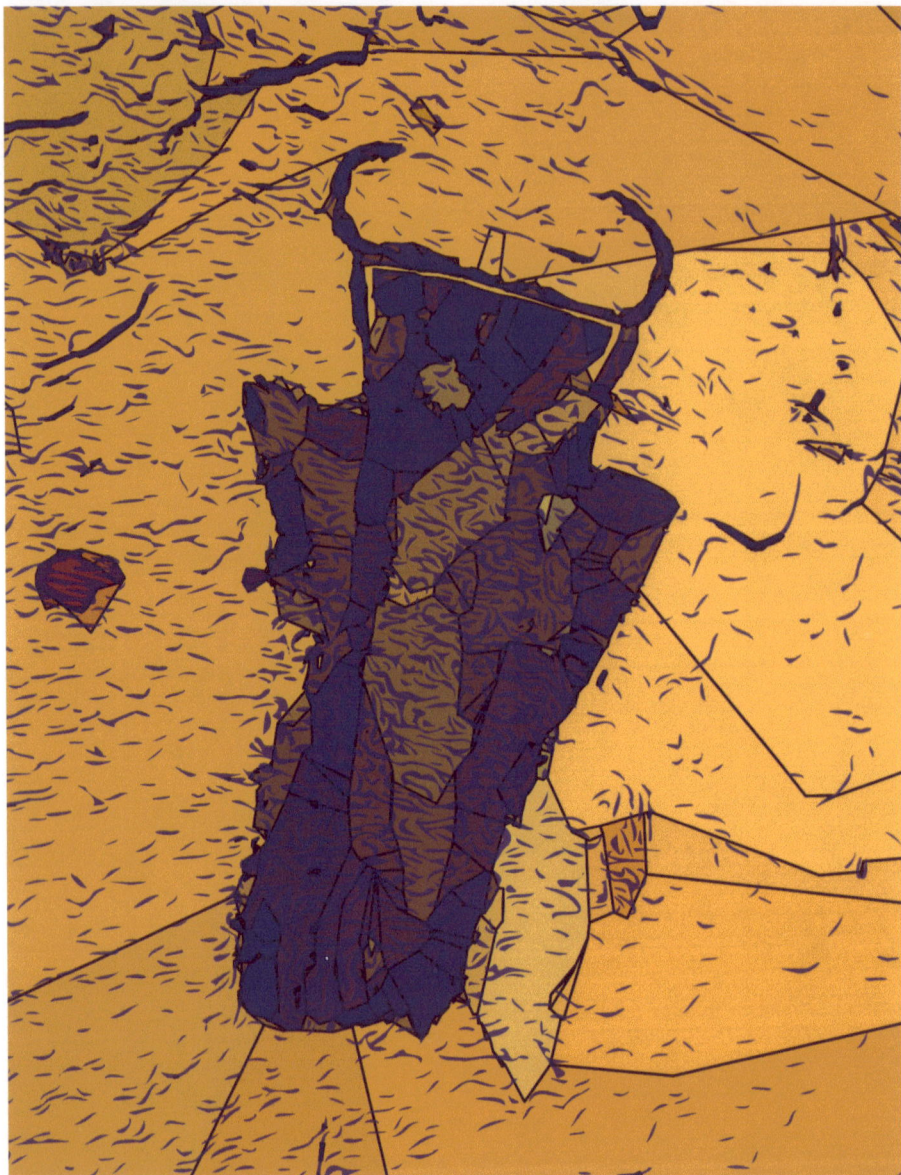

Calf creek rock art

Park History: Arches National Park

Arches National Park was established in 1971. It was the thirty-fourth National Park to be designated.

Arches National Park was designated a national monument by President Herbert Hoover in 1929. Later, on November 12, 1971, it was upgraded to a National Park.

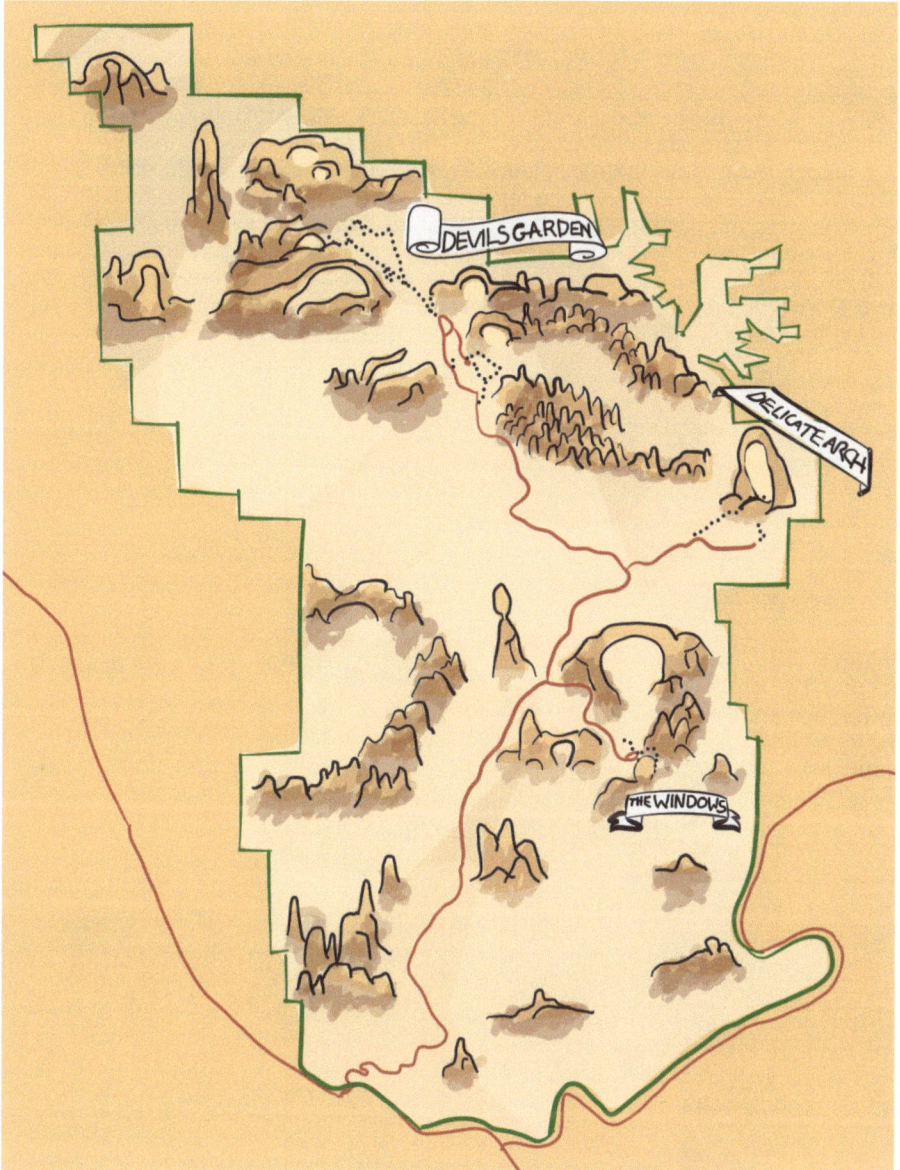

Campground

Devil's Garden Campground
2282 S. West Resources Blvd, Moab, UT 84532-0907
(435) 719-2299
38.7769444, -109.5891667

Day 41 *Activities*

HIKE: Devil's Garden
7.9 mi 1223' elv 5:00 DIFFICULT

Landscape Arch, six other main arches, and a large obelisk called Dark Angel can be reached by the main trail. The Primitive Loop is a difficult and less traveled way back.

Devils Garden Trail begins dramatically meandering amongst large sandstone formations. The first downhill spur on the right leads to Tunnel and Pine Tree Arches. Back on the main trail continue to Landscape Arch, the longest arch in North America. After Landscape Arch, the terrain is more challenging. Ascend up a fin where you can see Partition Arch, two arches side by side. A few minutes later turn left at the intersection to get to Partition Arch, and Navajo Arch. Back on the main trail again, follow rock cairns over a section of slick rock, and ascend another large, long sandstone fin. The end of the fin brings you to Black Arch Overlook and a bit farther to Double O Arch, two arches aligned vertically. Dark Angel is a .4 mile spur to a 125-foot tall solo obelisk rising abruptly out of the desert landscape. Retrace your steps to the four-way intersection at Double O Arch, and turn left on to Primitive Loop Trail. Along this section of trail hikers are scarce, route finding more difficult, and a few steep sandstone descents can be tricky. About a half mile farther up the trail, a short spur to the right takes you to the last arch, Private Arch. The rest of the loop to the Devils Garden Trail connector traverses a beautiful desert landscape that you may have all to yourself.

Location
The trailhead is .3 miles from the campground.

Feature	Distance	Time
Trailhead	0.3	0:07
Landscape Arch	0.8	0:20
Double O Arch	2.1	0:45
Dark Angel	2.5	1:00
Return via Primitive Loop	5.9	3:30
Trail to Pine Tree and Tunnel arches add	0.5	0:30
Trails to Navajo and Partition arches add	0.8	1:00
TOTAL DISTANCE ALL TRAILS	7.7	5:00

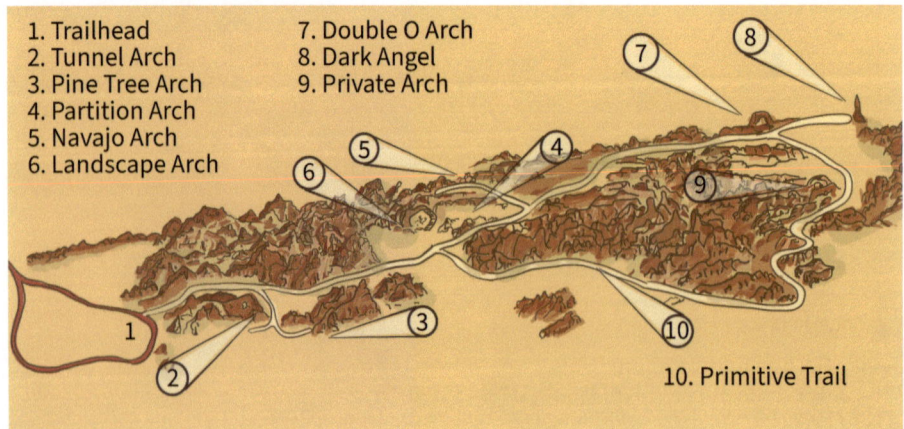

1. Trailhead
2. Tunnel Arch
3. Pine Tree Arch
4. Partition Arch
5. Navajo Arch
6. Landscape Arch
7. Double O Arch
8. Dark Angel
9. Private Arch
10. Primitive Trail

Arches National Park, UT - Mesa Verde National Park, CO

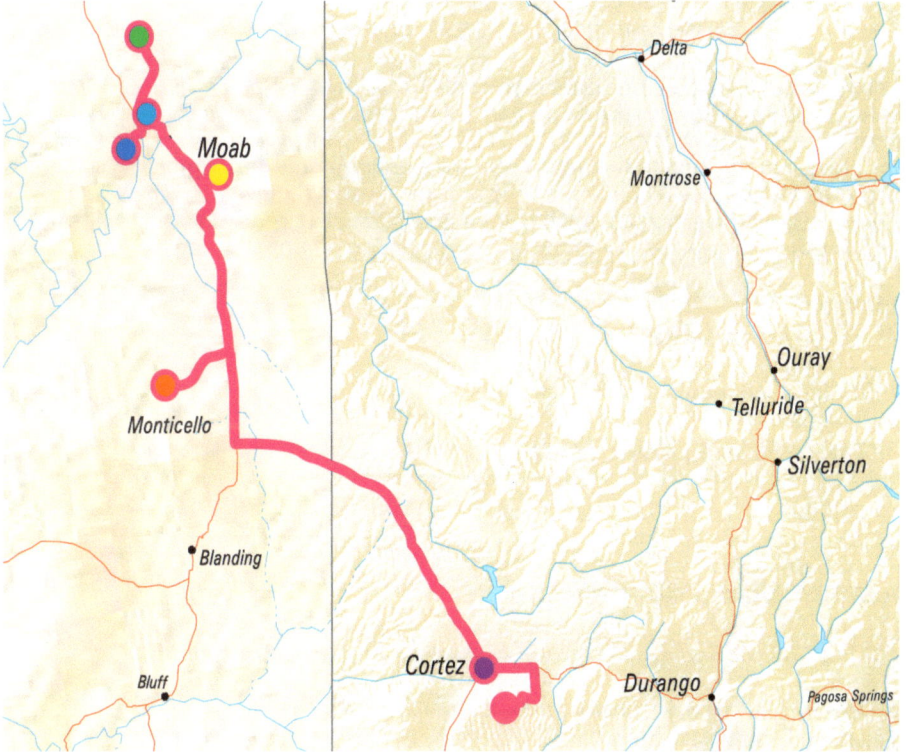

LOCATION	DISTANCE	TIME
● Arches National Park, UT	0 mi	0:00
● Windows Loop, UT	11 mi	0:20
● Courthouse Wash Rock, UT	20 mi	0:40
● Potash Road Petroglyphs, UT	24 mi	0:45
● Mill Creek Canyon, UT	45 mi	1:00
● Newspaper Rock, UT	97 mi	2:00
● RESUPPLY: Cortez, CO	185 mi	3:30
● Far View Lodge, CO	210 mi	4:10
Total	210 mi	4:10

Lodging

Far View Lodge
Mile Marker 15 Mesa Verde National Park, CO 81330
(970) 529-4465
37.2583106, -108.49368

Spotted Owl

Day 42 *Activities*

HIKE: Windows and Turret Arch
1.2 mi 154' elv :30 EASY

The Windows Loop is a collection of three separate short trails that all connect.

The Windows Trail and the Turret Arch Trail form a loop. At North Window, the trail splits to continue toward the North and South Windows, as well as the Primitive Loop. To see both, go left to hike out and back to the North Window Arch, returning for the rest of the loop to the right. From the North Window-Turret junction go left to continue around The Windows Loop Trail to the South Window Arch. The Windows Primitive Loop Trail begins, which follows around the backside of both the North and South Windows. Double Arch Trail can be added on from the same parking area.

Location
38.6871271, -109.5368942

HISTORY: Courthouse Wash Rock

Archaic-era Indians painted the petroglyphs between 1,500 and 4,000 years ago.

Location
38.6068536, -109.5876199

HISTORY: Potash Road Petroglyphs

The Potash Road Petroglyphs are not a hike but a road side attraction.

Archaeologists believe that the petroglyphs were done by Indians of the Southern San Rafael Fremont culture, which flourished between 600 A.D. and 1300 A.D.

Location
38.5333653, -109.6076828

SWIM: Mill Creek Canyon
1.2 mi 170' elv :30 EASY

Less than 5 minutes from the trailhead is a sandstone gorge below a small dam that provides a great place to hang out a short distance from the car. 20-30 minutes from the trailhead, you will arrive in Shangri-la, a large pool and waterfall.

Location
38.5617293, -109.5169710

HISTORY: Newspaper Rock

Newspaper Rock has petroglyphs dating back about 2000 years, to B.C. times. The panel is a mix of Navajo, Anasazi, and Fremont Indian creation.

Location
37.9882667, -109.5182

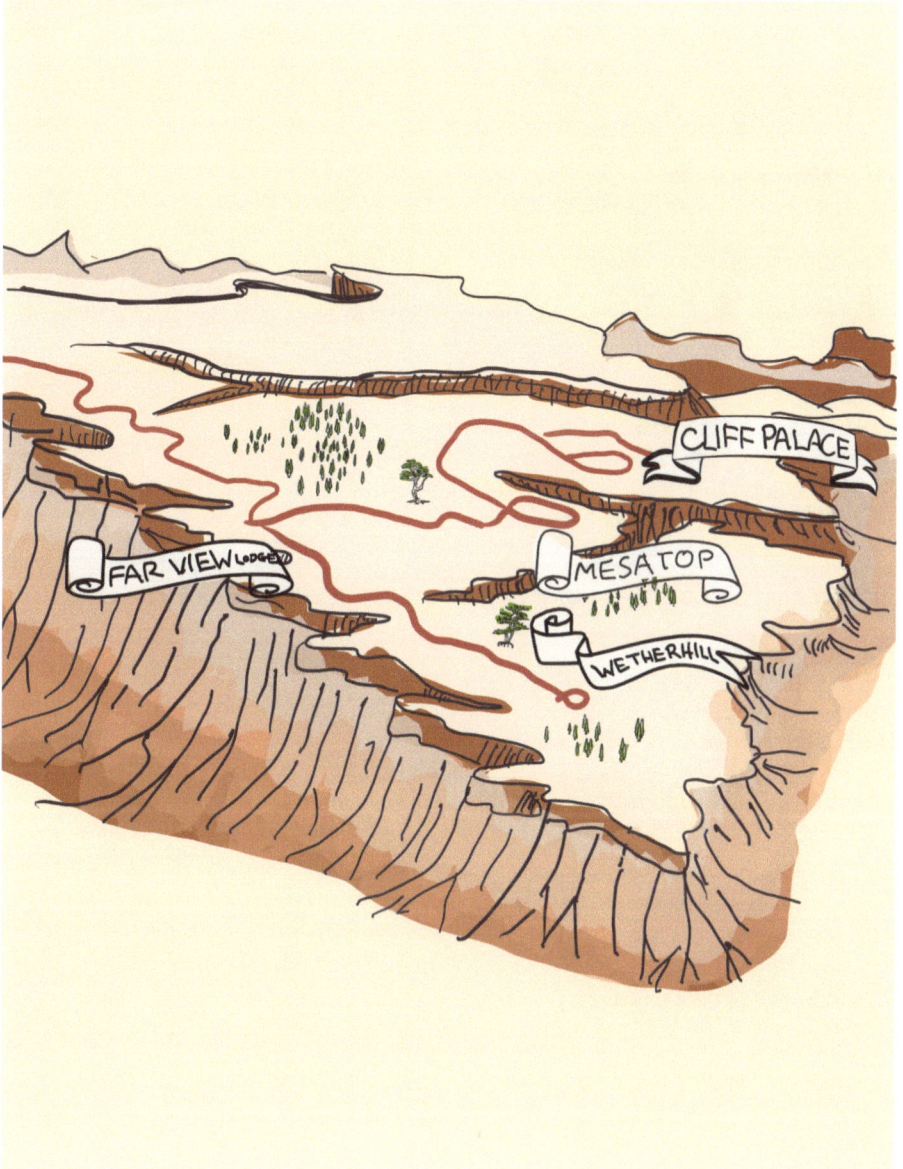

Lodging

Far View Lodge
Mile Marker 15 Mesa Verde National Park, CO 81330
(970) 529-4465
37.2583106, -108.49368

Day 43 *Activities*

HIKE: Cliff Palace
.25 mi 100' elv :45 EASY

Tour starts with stairs down the cliff. Guided tour of dwellings.

Location
37.1662526, -108.4723145

TOUR: Balcony House
.25 mi 100' elv :45 MODERATE

The tour starts by descending 130 step staircase then traversing to ascend a 35' ladder and 2 smaller ladders before entering the cliff dwelling. To exit you must crawl through an 18" wide by 12' long tunnel then ascend a 60' staircase with chain handrail before climbing 2 18' exposed wooden ladders.

Location
37.1619333, -108.4649562

TOUR: Long House
2.25 mi 150' elv 2:30 MODERATE

This tour is ranger assisted not guided with rangers posted at several locations along the way. Longer than most tours but is less difficult descending on a paved trail.

Location
37.1619333, -108.4649562

HIKE: Step House
1 mi 165' elv :45 MODERATE

A trail leads into Step House ruins located at Wetherhill Mesa near Long House.

Location
37.1958300, -108.5379803

TOUR: Square Tower House
1 mi 120' elv 1:30 HARD

Requires descending two 16' ladders and traversing a 34' long narrow cliff ledge.

Location
37.166880, -108.492858

HIKE: Far View Sites
.75 mi 0' elv :30 EASY

Visit the Mesa Top community on Chapin Mesa.

Location

History: Cliff Palace

Cliff Palace is one of the most elaborate cliff dwellings built at Mesa Verde. It served as the administrative center for a series of more than sixty dwellings around the mesa.

Around AD 550, some of the people living in the Four Corners region decided to move onto the Mesa Verde. For over 700 years these people lived on the mesa, eventually building elaborate communities in the sheltered alcoves of the canyon walls.

Their basic construction material was sandstone that they shaped into rectangular blocks about the size of a loaf of bread. The mortar between the blocks was a mix of dirt and water. Living rooms averaged about six feet by eight feet, space enough for two or three people. Isolated rooms in the rear and on the upper levels were generally used for storing crops. Settlements where constructed by individual family groups each with their own Kiva. Cliff Palace grew to include 150 rooms and twenty-three kivas. Individual family groups worked together as a collective sharing duties of farming corn and processing flour that was stored in the lower levels beneath the cliff dwelling. Intricate irrigation ditches were developed that collected and distributed water from cliff-side springs to the terraced farming areas.

In the late 1200s, Cliff Palace and all other dwellings were abandoned. There is no hard evidence as to why they moved away but it is most likely, that their population exceeded the resources of the area and the people had to move to areas more suitable to supporting their needs.

History: The Kiva

What makes a kiva unique from other structures is that they include a feature called a Sipapu, a small hole representing the "place of emergence" from the previous world.

According to Hopi oral tradition, this hole represents the place where Ancestral Pueblo people emerged from the previous world to this one. Much like the biblical story of Noah's Ark, Hopis believe that the world before this one was destroyed, but a few chosen people were saved.

"Throughout the year, kivas are used for the same purposes that they were in the time of the ancestors. Our religious leaders go into the kivas for days and weeks at a time to prepare. Kivas are used for our religious dances, ceremonies, celebrations, and annual gatherings, such as feast days. They are sacred places. I hope that all will be respectful and appreciate the importance kivas have for us."

-TJ Atsye, Laguna Pueblo

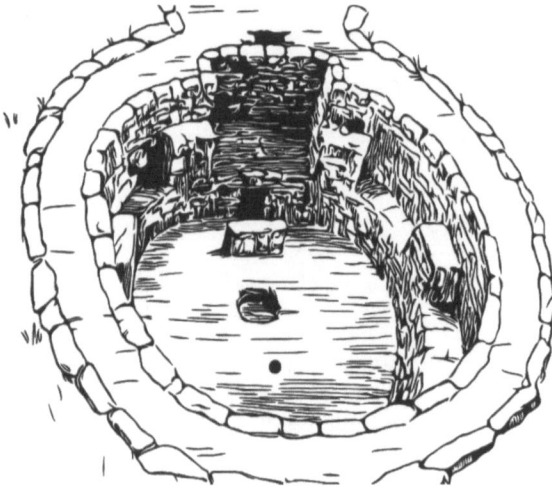

Park History: Mesa Verde National Park

Mesa Verde National Park was established in 1906. It was the seventh National Park to be designated.

Local ranchers first reported the cliff dwellings in the 1880s and soon archeologists and treasure hunters began combing the area for artifacts. The area that was once so well preserved by the arid desert climate and overhanging cliff walls was getting degraded rapidly. In response, a movement developed in the 1890s and early 1900s to make Mesa Verde a national park and to pass the Antiquities Act (1906) to prevent looting and vandalism at prehistoric sites on public land.

Day 44

Mesa Verde National Park, CO - Bogan Flats, CO

LOCATION	DISTANCE	TIME
🟢 Mesa Verde, CO	0 mi	0:00
🔵 Pinkerton Hot Springs, CO	64 mi	1:20
🔵 Box canyon falls Park, CO	118 mi	2:40
🟡 Penny Hot Spring, CO	254 mi	5:00
🔴 Bogan Flats Campground, CO	264 mi	5:15
Total	264 mi	5:15

Campground

Bogan Flats Campground
Marble, CO
(877) 444-6777
39.0997222, -107.2583333

Mountain Lion

Day 44 *Activities*

SOAK: Pinkerton Hot Spring

A colorful travertine formation spouts hot water from its geothermal source.

Roadside with parking within 25' of spring that hosts a small tub cut into the mineral deposits. Due to its proximity to the road most people simply view this as a beautiful feature, but the brave can soak in its high mineral content waters.

Location
35554 US-550, Durango, CO 81301
37.4510, -107.8053

HIKE: Box Canyon Falls Park
.5 mi 156' elv :30

Box Canyon Falls plummets through the very narrow quartzite gorge of Canyon Creek as it descends to the Uncompahgre River near Ouray.

An easy 500 foot walk into the thundering waterfalls! With access to the high bridge, perimeter trail, and nature center. This is a heavily developed park with an entrance fee.

Location
38.0182723, -107.6773007

SOAK: Penny Hot Spring

Several riverside pools resided beside the Crystal River in a mountainous ravine.

Roadside hot springs with parking within 125' of the spring which is down the bank on the edge of a river. Due to its proximity to the road this area can get very busy especially around sunset.

Location
10 mi North of Bogan Flats
39.23186, -107.22733

Tips: Poison Sumac

Poison sumac and oak are shrubs. Poison ivy usually grows as a vine on tree trunks or straggling over the ground. They all can cause allergic reactions that itch like crazy.

What to do?

Remove any clothing that has touched the plant. Gently wash skin and scrub under fingernails right away with water and mild soap or dish soap. For itching: Add oatmeal to the bath and put calamine lotion on the skin (but not on the face or on the genitals).

Bogan Flats, CO - Rocky Mountain National Park, CO

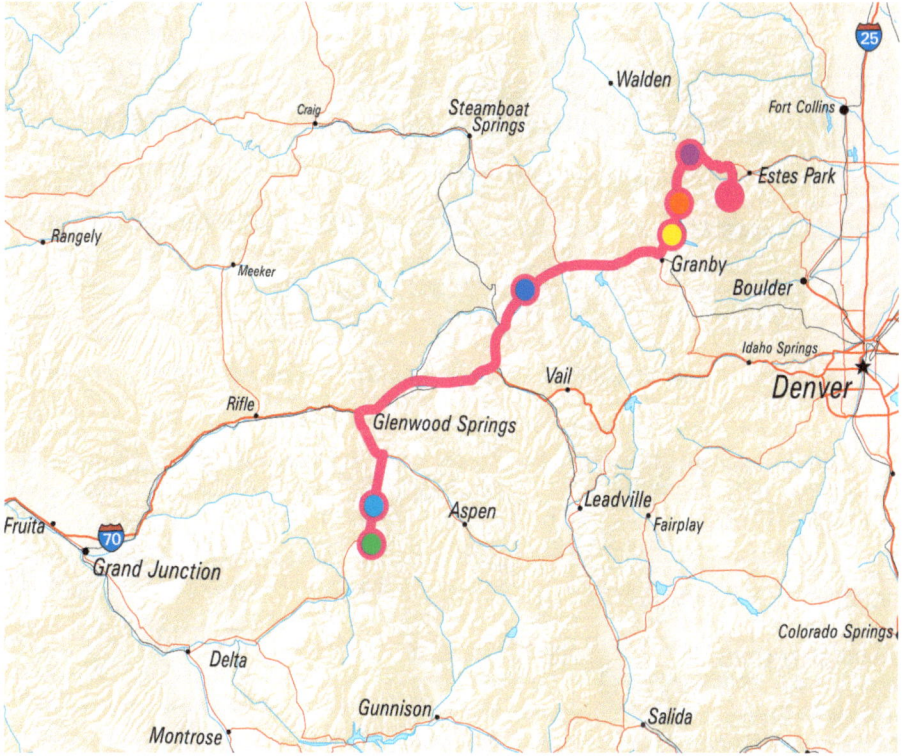

LOCATION	DISTANCE	TIME
🟢 Bogan Flats, CO	0 mi	0:00
🔵 Penny Hot Springs, CO	10 mi	0:15
🔵 Radium Hot Springs, CO	104 mi	2:15
🟡 Kawuneeche Visitors center, CO	160 mi	3:30
🟠 Lake Irene Picnic Area, CO	176 mi	4:00
🟣 Alpine Visitors Center, CO	182 mi	4:15
🔴 Glacier Basin Campground, CO	201 mi	5:15
Total	201 mi	5:15

Campground

Glacier Basin Campground
Highway 36 West, Estes Park, CO 80517
(970) 586-1206
40.3291667, -105.5933333

Wolverine

Day 45 *Activities*

SOAK: Radium Hot Spring
1.5mi 311' elv :45 MODERATE

Radium Hot Springs is a primitive warm springs pool located on the banks of the Colorado River.

The hike is a fairly flat trail until the descent down to the river where the warm springs are located. The climb down can be challenging for some.

Location
39.9512896, -106.5424017

HIKE: Adams Falls
.8 mi 104' elv :30 EASY

Adams Falls is a towering waterfall in Rocky Mountain National Park that eventually feeds into Grand Lake.

After a short walk on the wide popular path, you reach the loop for the falls. Follow the signs to the viewing area. The cascading water gains momentum as it drops, then takes a 90 degree turn into a rift in the rock forming many pools below.

Location
40.2395771, -105.8000836

HIKE: Lake Irene
.8 mi 85' elv :20 EASY

Have lunch at the picnic area, then enjoy a lovely stroll down to a pretty lake and an overlook.

From the picnic area at the historic cabin, you'll work your way down a gentle grade past a flowering, marshy meadow. Upon reaching the lake, the trail follows the shoreline with a small meadow on one side of this otherwise forested lake. Continue past the lake to an overlook for views looking down towards the Kawuneeche Valley.

Location
40.4139946, -105.8189439

HIKE: Alpine Ridge Trail
.6 mi 134' elv :30 MODERATE

This interpretive path gives you a sprawling view of the alpine areas around the visitors center.

The trail begins climbing right away from Fall River Pass, taking your breath away in the thin alpine air. At the top of the knoll, enjoy fantastic 360 degree panoramas.

Location
40.4411434, -105.7553591

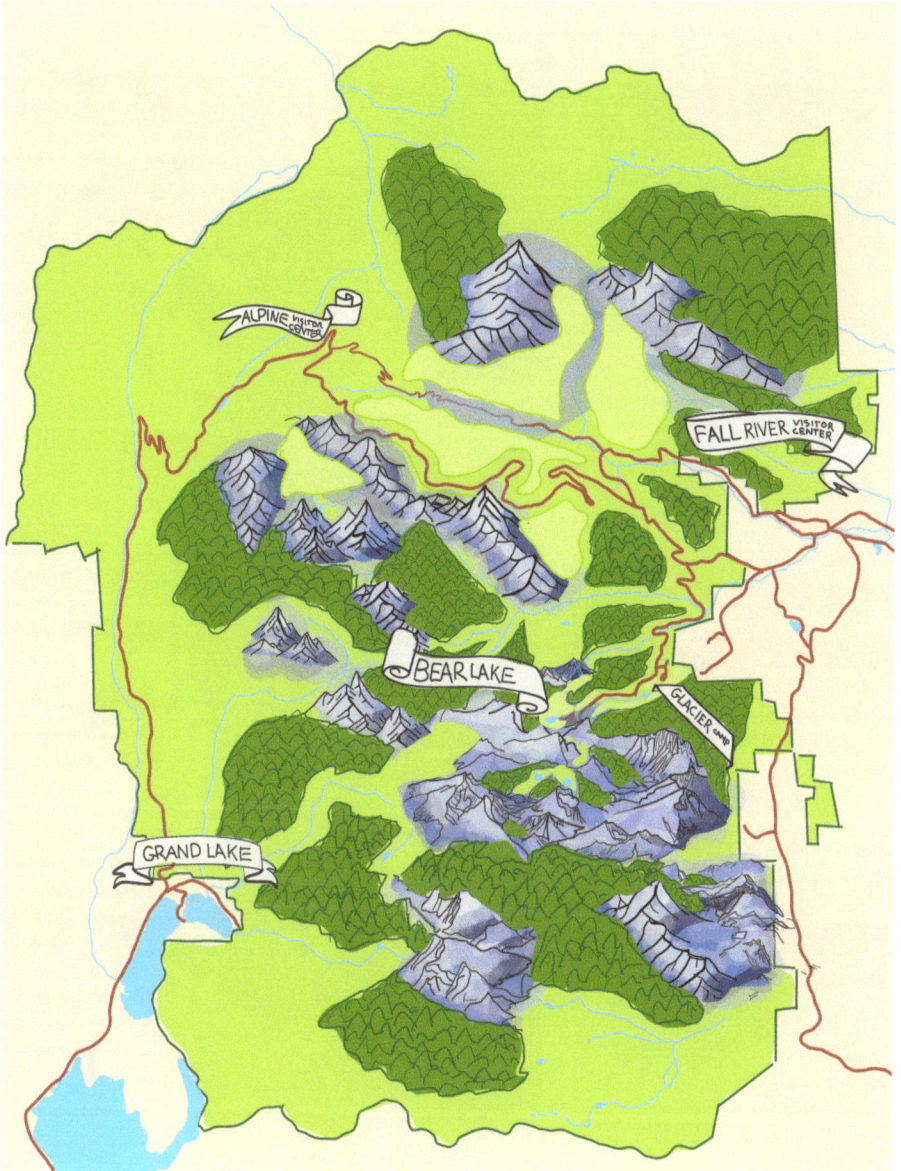

Campground

Glacier Basin Campground
Highway 36 West, Estes Park, CO 80517
(970) 586-1206
40.3291667, -105.5933333

Glacier Basin

FEATURE

1. Bear Lake
2. Dream Lake
3. Emerald Lake
4. Lake Haiyaha
5. Alberta Falls
6. The Loch
7. Timberline Falls
8. Lake of Glass
9. Sky Pond
10. Andrews Pond
11. Andrews Glacier
12. Mills Lake
13. Bierstadt Lake
14. Sprauge Lake

Day 46 *Activities*

HIKE: Emerald Lake
3.2 mi 702' elv 2:00 MODERATE

The trail to Emerald Lake offers maximum payoff for minimum effort making it the crown jewel of Rocky Mountain National Park.

From the ranger station begin walking west toward Bear Lake. In a couple hundred feet you'll pass a junction that leads down to the Glacier Gorge Trail. Keep to the right and head uphill. This section of trail is partially paved, and in a half mile you'll arrive at Nymph Lake, a small body of water surrounded by trees.On the north side of Nymph Lake, there is a small trail leading down to a bench beside the lake. The trail continues up the hill alongside a large rock outcropping and then at three quarters of a mile it reaches a switchback that sends you south up a section of stairs. At the top of these stairs on your left side is a terrific overlook out over Nymph Lake and into Glacier Gorge with Longs Peak standing high above it.

The trail continues up through aspen trees. At the first switchback you may notice a small cascade at the end of a short detour trail. At exactly one mile you'll reach a junction for Lake Haiyaha. Stay to the right and cross a log bridge across the outlet stream. Just beyond the bridge you'll climb a small rise and the main Dream Lake viewpoint will be on your left. From Dream Lake the trail follows the north shore and at 1.2 miles you'll cross a wooden boardwalk over a marshy area. At about 1.4 miles you'll reach the end of Dream Lake and will hear the inlet stream coming down from Emerald Lake. The trail now starts to climb somewhat steeply. As you climb you'll see a few small cascades and even a little waterfall. After this the trail winds up an area of rock steps before beginning its descent to Emerald Lake.

Feature	Distance	Time
Bear Lake	0.0	0:00
Nymph Lake	0.5	0:20
Dream Lake	1.1	0:45
Emerald Lake	1.8	1:15

Location
40.3119367, -105.6455887

Tips: Altitude Sickness

Drink more water than usual and rest for a day when you exceed 2,000' of elevation change in a day when traveling above 8,000'. DO NOT DRINK ALCOHOL.

Acute mountain sickness (AMS) can develop within hours after ascending to a higher altitude. Symptoms may include headache, insomnia, irritability, dizziness, muscle aches, fatigue, loss of appetite, nausea, vomiting, and swelling of the face, hands and feet. Descend before symptoms get worse. Acclimate for a day before ascending.

Severe forms of altitude sickness are high altitude cerebral edema (HACE) and high altitude pulmonary edema (HAPE). Danger signs of severe altitude sickness include severe headache, extreme fatigue or breathlessness (especially while resting), and any neurological problems such as stumbling, confusion, poor judgment or changes in consciousness. HACE and HAPE are medical emergencies and may result in coma or even death. It is crucial to descend and receive drug and oxygen therapy as soon as possible.

Park History: Rocky Mountain National Park

Rocky Mountain National Park was established in 1915. It was the ninth National Park to be designated.

Although never a year-round home, the Ute tribe utilized the areas green valleys, tundra meadows, and crystal lakes. The Utes dominated the area until the late 1700s. In 1843, explorer Rufus Sage wrote the first account of the Rocky's natural wonders, called Scenes in the Rocky Mountains. In 1859 the Pikes Peak gold rush drew miners to the area. When the park was created in 1915, private lands dotted the park and many hosted lodges, maintained roads, built trails, and guided visitors into the high country. As visitation increased after World War I, the simple park facilities and private lodges became inadequate. Rangers built comfort stations, museums, and well-maintained trails to meet the increasing demands of tourists.

During the 1930s, the National Park Service built Trail Ridge Road. The CCC also constructed campgrounds and trails to make the park accessible to a wide variety of tourists. In 1966, the 50th anniversary of the National Park Service. A new kind of centralized facility, called a Visitors Center, was created in Rocky Mountain National Park. It was at this time under the name Mission 66 that the National Park Service acquired many of the old guest lodges within the park boundaries, removed all the buildings and built new campgrounds and parking lots.

The RMNP shuttle system was created in 1978 to reduce the environmental impact of increased visitation that had caused parking lots to overflow.

RMNP Shuttle System

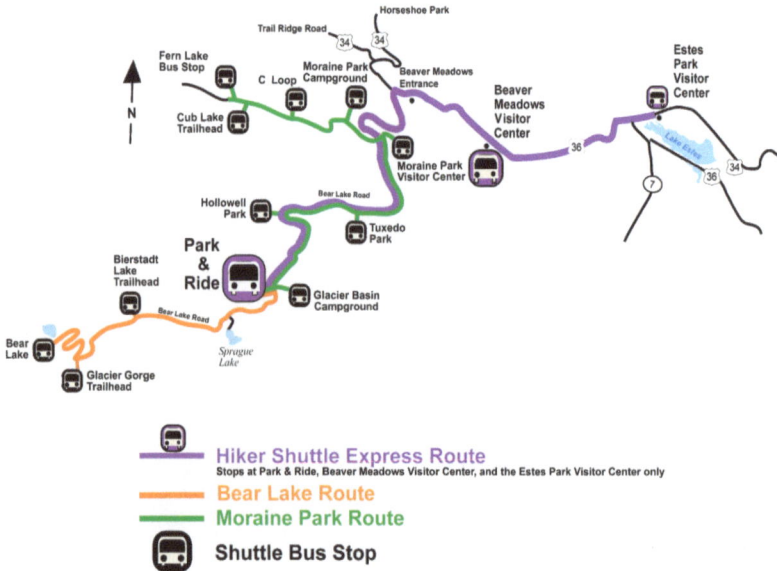

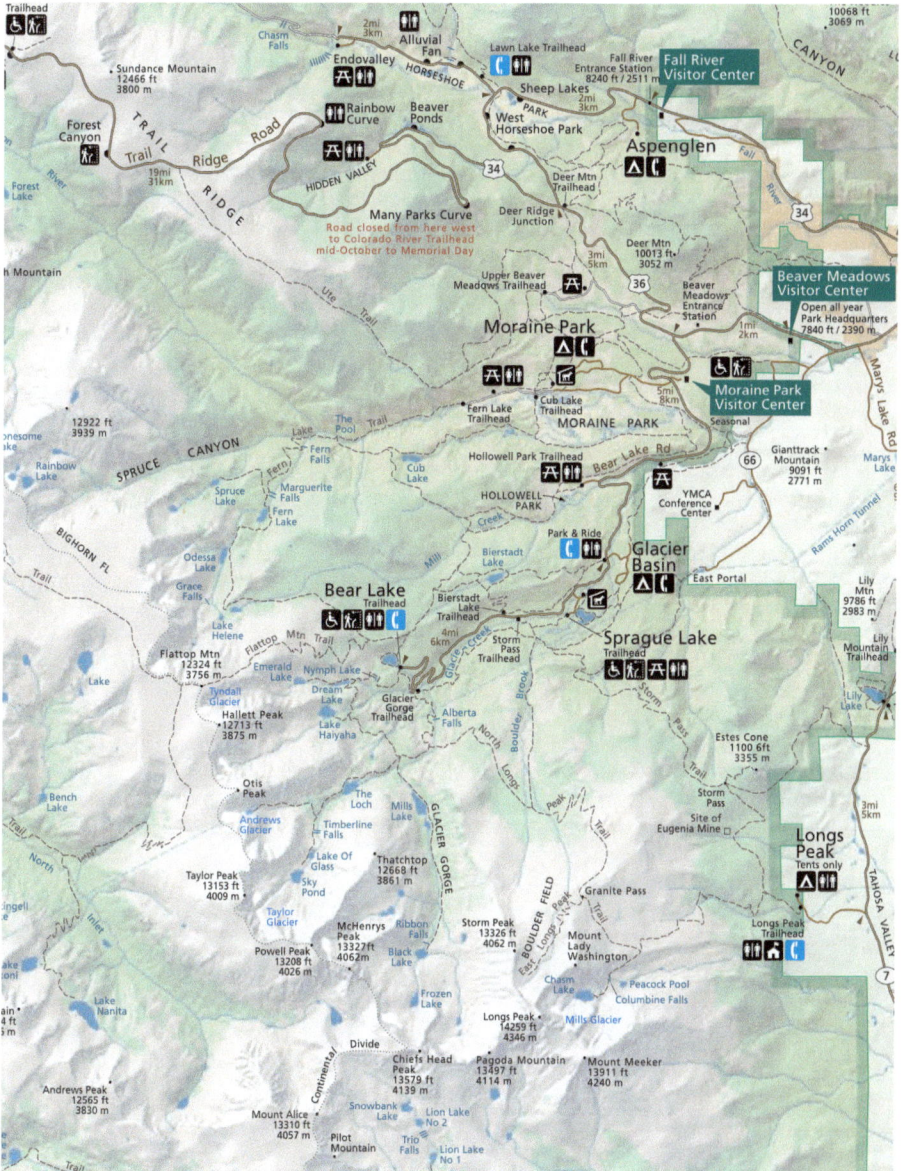

Trailhead

10068 ft / 3069 m

Chasm Falls · 2mi 3km · Alluvial Fan · Lawn Lake Trailhead · Fall River Entrance Station 8240 ft / 2511 m · Fall River Visitor Center · CANYON

Sundance Mountain 12466 ft 3800 m · Endovalley · HORSESHOE

Forest Canyon · TRAIL Ridge Road · Rainbow Curve · Beaver Ponds · Sheep Lakes · 2mi 3km · West Horseshoe Park · PARK

Forest River · 19mi 31km · RIDGE · HIDDEN VALLEY · 34 · Deer Mtn Trailhead · Aspenglen · Fall River · 34

Forest Lake

Many Parks Curve
Road closed from here west to Colorado River Trailhead mid-October to Memorial Day · Deer Ridge Junction · Deer Mtn 10013 ft 3052 m · 3mi 5km

h Mountain · Ute Trail · Upper Beaver Meadows Trailhead · 36 · Beaver Meadows Entrance Station · Beaver Meadows Visitor Center · Open all year Park Headquarters 7840 ft / 2390 m

Moraine Park · Moraine Park Visitor Center · 1mi 2km · Seasonal · Marys Lake Rd

12922 ft 3939 m · The Pool · Fern Lake Trailhead · Cub Lake Trailhead · MORAINE PARK · 5mi 8km

nesome ke · Lake Trail · SPRUCE CANYON · Fern Falls · Cub Lake · Hollowell Park Trailhead · Bear Lake Rd · 66 · Gianttrack Mountain 9091 ft 2771 m · Marys Lake

Rainbow Lake · Spruce Lake · Marguerite Falls · Fern Lake · HOLLOWELL PARK · Creek · YMCA Conference Center

BIGHORN FL · Odessa Lake · Mill · Bierstadt Lake · Park & Ride · Glacier Basin · East Portal · Rams Horn Tunnel · Lily Mtn 9786 ft 2983 m

Grace Falls · Bear Lake Trailhead · Bierstadt Lake Trailhead

Lake Helene · Flattop Mtn Trail · 4mi 6km · Storm Pass Trailhead · Sprague Lake Trailhead · Lily Mountain Trailhead

Flattop Mtn 12324 ft 3756 m · Emerald Lake · Nymph Lake · Glacier Creek · Storm Pass · Lily Lake

Tyndall Glacier · Hallett Peak 12713 ft 3875 m · Dream Lake · Glacier Gorge Trailhead · Lake Haiyaha · Alberta Falls · North Boulder · Estes Cone 1100 6ft 3355 m

Bench Lake · Otis Peak · The Loch · Mills Lake · Longs Peak · Storm Pass · Site of Eugenia Mine · 3mi 5km

Andrews Glacier · Timberline Falls · GLACIER GORGE · Longs Peak Tents only · TAHOSA VALLEY

Lake Of Glass · Thatchtop 12668 ft 3861 m · BOULDER FIELD · Granite Pass · Longs Peak Trailhead

Taylor Peak 13153 ft 4009 m · Sky Pond

ngeli Inlet · Taylor Glacier · McHenrys Peak 13327ft 4062m · Ribbon Falls · Storm Peak 13326 ft 4062 m · Mount Lady Washington · 7

Powell Peak 13208 ft 4026 m · Black Lake · East Long's Peak · Chasm Lake · Peacock Pool · Columbine Falls

Lake Nanita · Frozen Lake · Longs Peak 14259 ft 4346 m · Mills Glacier

ain ke 4 ft 5 m · Divide · Chiefs Head Peak 13579 ft 4139 m · Pagoda Mountain 13497 ft 4114 m · Mount Meeker 13911 ft 4240 m

Andrews Peak 12565 ft 3830 m · Continental · Mount Alice 13310 ft 4057 m · Snowbank Lake · Lion Lake No 2

Pilot Mountain · Trio Falls · Lion Lake No 1 · Trail

Campground

Glacier Basin Campground
Highway 36 West, Estes Park, CO 80517
(970) 586-1206
40.3291667, -105.5933333

133

Day 47 *Activities*

HIKE: Alberta Falls, The Loch and Sky Pond
7.8 mi 1,973' elv 5:30 DIFFICULT

The views here are simply spectacular, passing waterfalls and visiting alpine lake that fill a cirque basin surrounded on three sides by sheer cliff walls.

Roughly one-quarter of a mile from the parking area, just after crossing Chaos Creek, the trail briefly converges with the Glacier Creek Trail. After a short distance the Glacier Creek Trail splits off to the right and heads toward Bear Lake. Turn left at this junction to continue to Sky Pond. At just over eight-tenths of a mile the trail reaches Alberta Falls. This beautiful 30-foot waterfall crashes down a narrow gorge carved by Glacier Creek. At 1.6 miles the route reaches the North Longs Peak Trail junction. Turn right and in about a half-mile up this trail you'll reach Mills Junction. Proceed straight ahead onto the Loch Vale Trail.

Above Mills junction the route gets very steep as it ascends a series of short switchbacks through an impressive gorge, while Icy Brook cascades down the valley. At the third switchback you'll reach a vantage point that offers a nice view of a waterfall tumbling down the gorge. At roughly 2.8 miles hikers will reach Loch Vale, better known as The Loch. Beyond the lake the trail begins to climb again, and at just over 3.6 miles you'll arrive at the Sky Pond / Andrews Glacier split. The trail to the right leads to Andrews Glacier. Stay to the left at this junction.

Roughly one-third of a mile above the junction you'll enjoy your first open view of Timberline Falls high above the trail. From this vantage point the trail begins to climb a series of rock steps roughly 200 feet in just 0.15 miles. At just over 4 miles from the trailhead hikers will arrive at the base of Timberline Falls. The trail continues up a chute to the right of the falls and soon becomes a challenging scramble that climbs roughly 100 feet, requiring the use of both hands and feet. The first 30 feet or so are the most difficult, but beyond that it's an easy scramble. At just over 4.1 miles from the trailhead, hikers will reach the Lake of Glass. From the lake the trail becomes rocky as it travels along the west shore. At roughly 4.5 miles hikers will finally arrive at Sky Pond, sitting at an elevation of 10,900 feet.

Feature	Distance	Time
Bear Lake	0.0	0:00
Alberta Falls	0.8	0:45
Loch Vale	2.8	2:15
Timberline Falls	4.0	3:00
Lake of Glass	4.1	3:15
Sky Pond	4.5	3:45

Location
40.3119367, -105.6455887

This parking area fills up extremely early. It is recommended to take the shuttle from the park and ride near Glacier Basin Campground.

Day 48

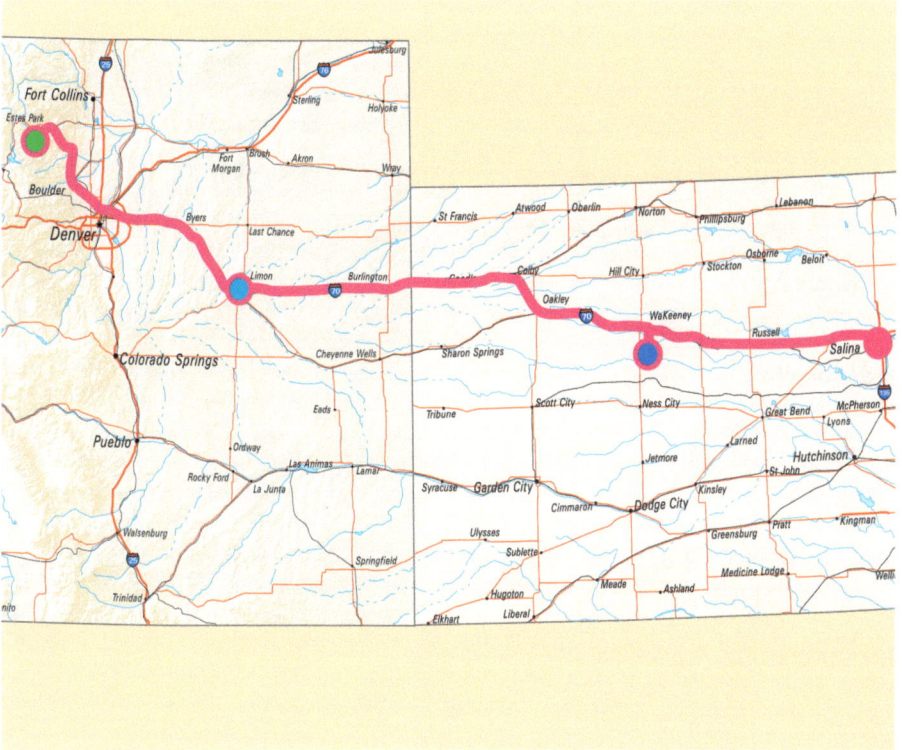

LOCATION	DISTANCE	TIME
🟢 Glacier Basin Campground, CO	0 mi	0:00
🔵 Limon Wetlands, CO	156 mi	2:45
🔵 Cedar Bluff State Park, KS	393 mi	6:00
🔴 Salina, KS	529 mi	8:00
Total	529 mi	8:00

Lodging

Country Inn and Suites by Radisson
2760 S. 9th St., Salina, KS, 67401
(785) 502-8062
38.789059, -97.615219

Great Blue Heron

Day 48 *Activities*

WALK: Limon Wetlands

A paved trail extends south half a mile to an interpretive kiosk and gazebo overlooking the wetlands.

Location
39.2594357, -103.6778095

WALK: Cedar Bluffs Overlook

A series of bluffs that overlook the Cedar Bluff Reservoir.

Location
38.7759, -99.80996

RESUPPLY: Aldi
2403 S Ninth St
Salina, KS 67401
38.79715, -97.61221

LOCATION	DISTANCE	TIME
🟢 Salina, KS	0 mi	0:00
🔵 Missouri Town Living History Museum, MO	200 mi	3:00
🔵 Ha Ha Tonka State Park, MO	353 mi	5:30
🔴 Johnson's Shut-Ins State Park, MO	510 mi	8:20
Total	510 mi	8:20

Campground

Johnson's Shut-Ins State Park
148 Taum Sauk Trail, Middle Brook, MO 63656
(573) 546-2450
37.54996517, -90.88851655

Ruffled Grouse

Day 49 *Activities*

HISTORY: Missouri Town Living History Museum

Missouri Town is a living history museum with more than 25 buildings dating from 1822 to 1860 spread across 30 acres.

Location
38.9728989, -94.3204691

WALK: Ha Ha Tonka State Park

This park features sinkholes, caves, a huge natural bridge, sheer bluffs, and the ruins of turn of the 20th century mansion.

Location
37.9762588, -92.7694425

SWIM: Shut-In's
2.4 mi 484' elv 2:00 EASY

A spectacular and popular series of cataracts and potholes that form an almost endless series of swimming holes.

A short trail down to the river brings you to this unique swimming area.

Location
37.54025, -90.84341

Day 50

Johnson's Shut-Ins, MO - Red River Gorge, KY

LOCATION	DISTANCE	TIME
🟢 Johnsons Shut Ins, MO	0 mi	0:00
🔵 Ferne Clyffe, IL	142 mi	3:00
🔵 Mammoth Cave , KY	350 mi	6:30
🔴 Middle Fork Campground, KY	540 mi	9:30
Total	540 mi	9:30

Campground

Middle Fork Campground
2135 Natural Bridge Rd, Slade, KY 40376
(606) 663-2214
37.76675072, -83.6749104

Chorus Frog

Day 50 *Activities*

HIKE: Ferne Clyffe Waterfall
1 mi 183' elv :30 EASY

Visit a 100' waterfall.

The Big Rocky Hollow Trail will take hikers to the Ferne Clyffe Waterfall. The main waterfall is 100-feet tall with a second level that has a large natural cave shelter. The trail also features additional smaller waterfalls, scenic creeks, bluffs and a beautiful hardwood forest.

Location
37.5429158, -88.9798138

TOUR: Mammoth Cave (Frozen Niagara)
.75 mi 64' elv 1:25

The Frozen Niagara Tour showcases the park's densest collection of stalactites and stalagmites.

The Frozen Niagara Tour requires a short bus ride from the Mammoth Cave Visitor Center and a short walk from the bus stop to the cave entrance. From there participants take a 32-step staircase to the bottom. Reservations are required.

Location
37.1874925, -86.1014951

HIKE: Cedar Sink Trail
1.5 mi 209' elv :45 EASY

The Cedar Sink Trail takes visitors 300 feet deep inside of a massive 7 acre sinkhole.

The first half mile of the trail is a relaxing hike through the dense woods of the park. This shady path makes two noticeable drops that will let you know that you're approaching the sinkhole. As you work your way down, you'll be able to admire sheer limestone cliff edges and outcrops all on a gentle boardwalk. The trail will make a short loop around the feature before returning to the trailhead.

Location
37.1555384, -86.1604875

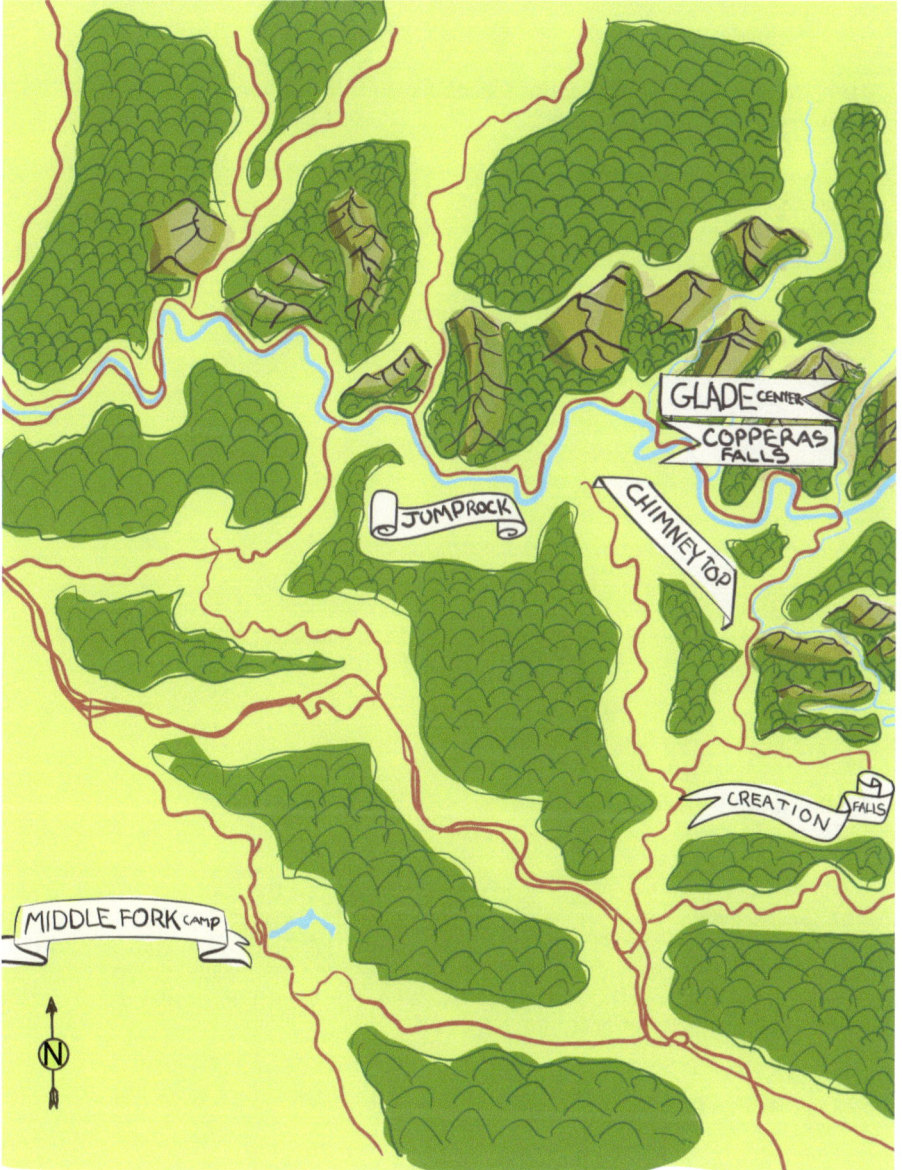

GLADE CENTER

COPPERAS FALLS

JUMPROCK

CHIMNEY TOP

CREATION FALLS

MIDDLE FORK CAMP

N

Campground

Middle Fork Campground
2135 Natural Bridge Rd, Slade, KY 40376
(606) 663-2214
37.76675072, -83.6749104

Day 51 *Activities*

SWIM: Red River Jump Rock
1 mi 25' elv :30 EASY

This is the swimming hole to visit in the gorge!

The trail follows along Red River until reaching the intersection with Sheltowee Trace at the footbridge.

Location
37.8249722, -83.6288611

MUSEUM: Gladie Cultural Center

Learn about the cultural heritage and geology of the area.

Location
37.83329468, -83.60774657

HIKE: Copperas Falls
3.5 mi 167' elv 1:30 MODERATE

Copperas falls spills 42 feet over a rock overhang into a sand beach pool below.

Follow the user trails along Copperas Creek to reach the falls. It is easiest to walk in the stream bed itself. When you get close, you'll see some large boulders with cut tree stumps between them right before you reach the falls.

Location
37.820917, -83.575719

HIKE: Chimney Top & Princess Arch
.5 mi 15' elv :15 EASY

Descend gently before reaching a wide intersection that is the start of the loop. Take the left turn and descend more before turning towards a view of Princess Arch. Continuing on the loop, you'll see Little Princess Arch which is a thin arch inside of a small rock overhang. Continuing on the loop, stay on the main wide path before circling back to the top of the arch with an overlook just short of the arch-top crossing. Walk uphill to return to the trailhead.

Location
37.824863167, -83.61827852

HIKE: Rock Bridge Creation Falls
1.5 mi 259' elv 1:00 EASY

Rock Bridge Trail #207 is paved loop trail that descends into a deep ravine with towering hemlock trees and dense rhododendron understory.

Location
37.769917, -83.566831

Red River Gorge, KY - Shenandoah National Park, VA

LOCATION		DISTANCE	TIME
🟢	Red River Gorge, KY	0 mi	0:00
🔵	Babcock State Park, WV	220 mi	4:15
🔵	Warm Springs, VA	316 mi	6:10
🔴	Big Meadows Campground, VA	427 mi	8:30
	Total	427 mi	8:30

Campground

Big Meadows Campground
3655 U.S. Highway 211 East, Luray, VA 22835
(540) 999-3500
38.5286194, -78.438725

Red Fox

Day 52 *Activities.*

HISTORY: Babcock State Park - Glade Creek Grist Mill

Babcock State Park features rock-hewn streams, rhododendron-lined trails, and a historic mill.

Beneath the historic grist mill is a short stone pathway that leads you to the beautiful cascades of Glade Creek Grist Mill Falls.

Location
37.9795808, -80.9463470

SOAK: Warm Springs, VA

Soak in a beautifully restored historic bath house.

Settlement of Warm Springs began in the mid-1700's. It centered on the natural springs that colonists had discovered while exploring the Virginia frontier. Word spread that the warm waters offered relief from various ailments and soon visitors began to travel to area to "take the waters."

Thomas Jefferson spent three weeks at the pools in 1819, bathing three times a day to relieve pain caused by rheumatism.

The Homestead Hotel is now owned by Omni Resorts and has restored the bath houses to offer soaking as either separate male and female or mixed bathing experiences depending on the hour.

Location
11 Bath St, Warm Springs, VA 24484
38.0540333, -79.7801121

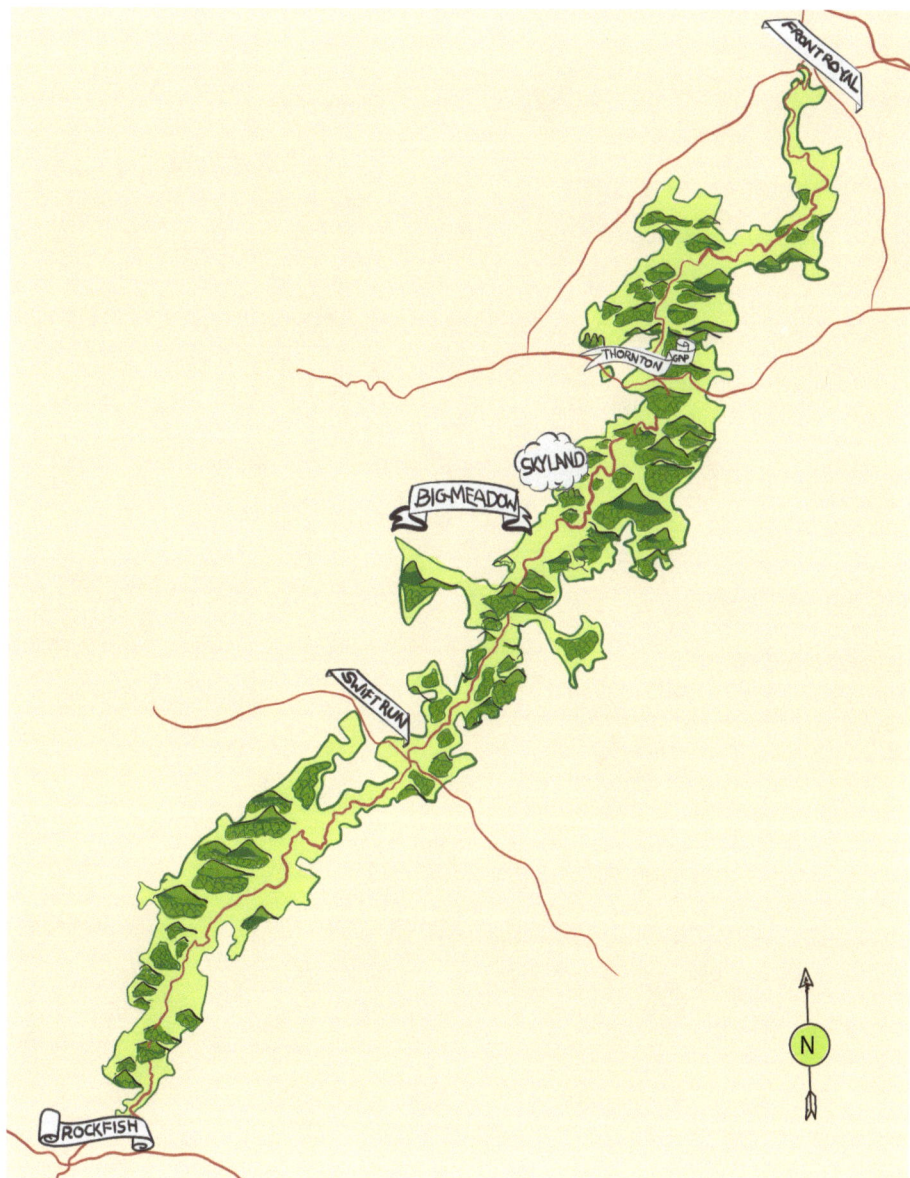

Campground

Big Meadows Campground
3655 U.S. Highway 211 East, Luray, VA 22835
(540) 999-3500
38.5286194, -78.438725

Big Meadows Area

FEATURE
1. Dark Hollow Falls
2. Rose River Falls
3. Big Meadows Lodge
4. Byrd Visitors Center
5. Lewis Falls Overlook

Day 53 *Activities.*

HIKE: Dark Hollow Falls Rose River Falls Loop
6.2 mi 1675' elv 3:45 MODERATE

Visit multiple waterfalls on this moderate loop from Big Meadows Campground.

Starting at the back of the campground take a left on the Appalachian trail. Look for a cement trail post with a white blaze at around one half of a mile. This will lead you to the Amphitheater and Park Office. Continue past the office and take the first right to "Big Meadows Loop A". Follow the road through the campground on Loop A and at campsite #18 take an unpaved path on the right. The path leads to the blue-blazed Story of the Forest Trail. Turn left here and leave the AT. Follow the Story of the Forest Trail until you reach Skyline Drive at 1.7 miles. Cross Skyline Drive and follow the blue-blazed Dark Hollow Falls trail on the left. The paved trail quickly ends and an unpaved path begins to steeply descend numerous sets of steps and switchbacks.

Reach the first view of the falls at 2.3 miles. A series of cascades and pools are formed by the 70' waterfall. Continue down the trail past more small pools and cataracts and reach the bridge and trail junction. On the right are some nice views of the lower falls. The bridge crosses Hogcamp Branch and then meets the blue-blazed Rose River Falls Loop trail on the left.

Take a left on the Rose River Loop Trail toward Fishers Gap. The trail follows the stream and the trail becomes more difficult. More small cataracts and pools are formed by the stream within easy access of the trail. A metal footbridge crosses Hogcamp Branch and then a small stream crossing is required. Continue on the trail and the Rose River soon joins on the right. Reach Rose River Falls at 4.1 miles. This 67' waterfall forms a small pool at its base and a steep spur trail leads to the bottom of the falls.

Continue the climb as the trail parallels the river hosting several pools. The trail soon leaves the river and the climb up continues. The trail joins the yellow-blazed Skyland-Big Meadows Horse Trail. Stay left on the combined trail to reach the Rose River Fire Road. Bear right here and cross Skyline Drive.

Stay to the right after crossing the road and enter a hiker parking lot, not the parking area for Fishers Gap that is on the left. Follow the parking area and meet the Appalachian Trail at the end of the parking area near the fire road gate. Take a left and follow the white-blazed AT southbound for 1.5 miles. Reach an open area with nice views to the west before entering the forest. The Big Meadows campground where you started the hike is on the left at 6.2 miles.

Feature	Distance	Time
Skyline Drive	1.7	0:45
Dark Hollow Falls	2.3	1:15
Rose River Falls	4.1	2:15
Skyline Drive AT	5.3	3:00
Big Meadows Campground	6.2	3:45

Park History: Shenandoah National Park

Shenandoah National Park was established in 1935. It was the twentieth National Park to be designated.

In 1923, National Park Service Director Stephen Mather approached Calvin Coolidge's Secretary of the Interior Hubert Work, with a request to establish a national park on the East Coast. In 1925 the Virginia Chamber of Commerce and Shenandoah Valley, Inc., formed the Shenandoah National Park Association, Inc. In order to collect funds and receive donated land for the proposed park.

From 1931-1933, Herbert Hoover, who had a fishing camp on the Rapidan River allocated public use funds to build the initial 32 miles of Skyline Drive connecting Hoover's Camp Rapidan, Big Meadows, Skyland, and Thornton Gap. The CCC developed trails, picnic areas, overlooks, Skyline Drive features, water and sewer systems, comfort stations and drinking fountains. Development was taking place but many of the legal and financial hurdles of securing land kept the park from being established until 1935.

Skyland

Decades before Shenandoah National Park was established, vacationers traveled to Skyland Resort seeking an escape from urban life. The Skyland Resort became the core of the new Shenandoah National Park after the National Park Service awarded the new concession contract to Virginia Sky-Line Company, Inc. in 1937.

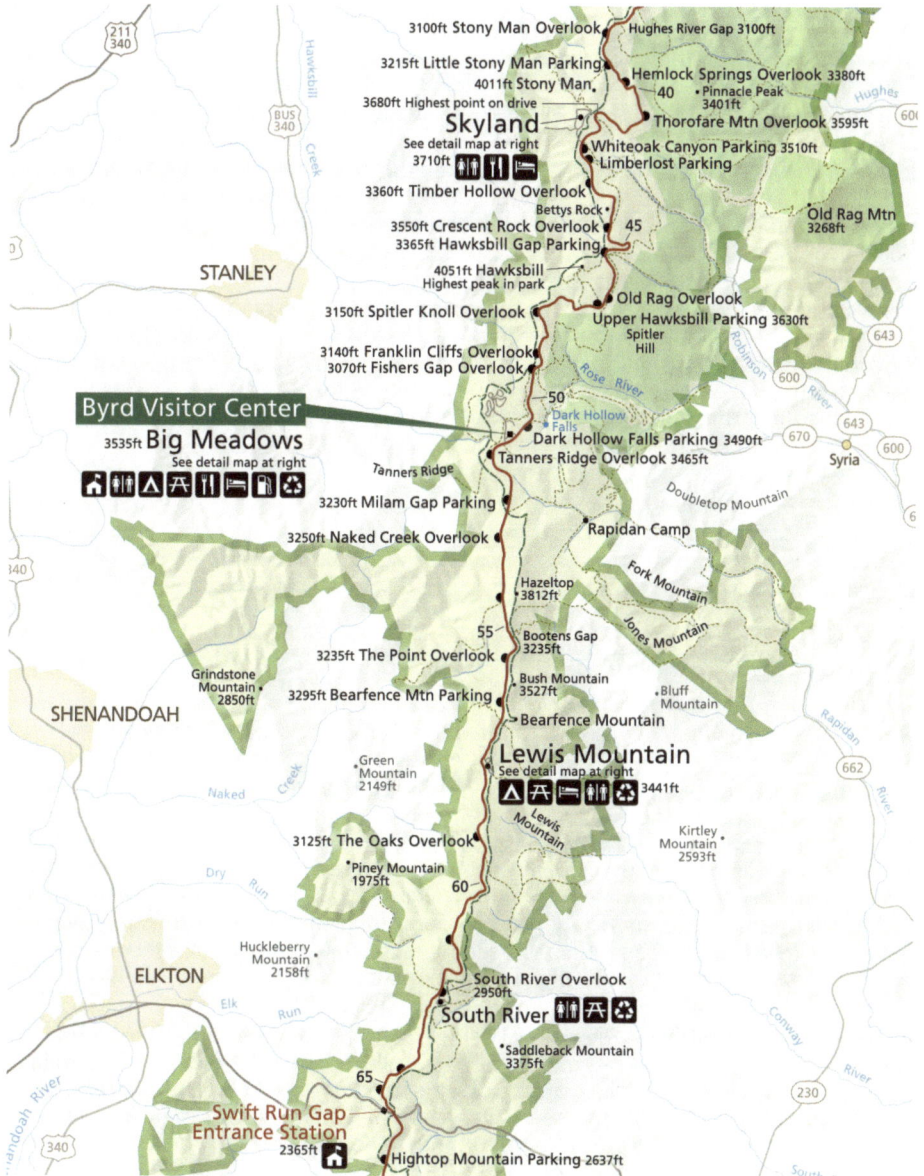

3100ft Stony Man Overlook — Hughes River Gap 3100ft

3215ft Little Stony Man Parking
4011ft Stony Man
Hemlock Springs Overlook 3380ft
40 • Pinnacle Peak 3401ft
3680ft Highest point on drive
Thorofare Mtn Overlook 3595ft
Skyland
See detail map at right
Whiteoak Canyon Parking 3510ft
3710ft 🚻 🍴 🛏
Limberlost Parking

3360ft Timber Hollow Overlook
Bettys Rock •
Old Rag Mtn 3268ft
3550ft Crescent Rock Overlook
3365ft Hawksbill Gap Parking
45
4051ft Hawksbill
Highest peak in park
Old Rag Overlook
3150ft Spitler Knoll Overlook
Upper Hawksbill Parking 3630ft
Spitler Hill
3140ft Franklin Cliffs Overlook
3070ft Fishers Gap Overlook
Rose River

STANLEY

Byrd Visitor Center
3535ft **Big Meadows**
See detail map at right
🏠 🚻 ⛺ 🎏 🍴 🛏 🛒 ♻
50
Dark Hollow Falls
Dark Hollow Falls Parking 3490ft
Tanners Ridge Overlook 3465ft
Tanners Ridge

3230ft Milam Gap Parking

3250ft Naked Creek Overlook

Rapidan Camp

Hazeltop 3812ft
Doubletop Mountain
Fork Mountain

55
Bootens Gap 3235ft
3235ft The Point Overlook
Jones Mountain
Bush Mountain 3527ft
Grindstone Mountain 2850ft
3295ft Bearfence Mtn Parking
• Bluff Mountain
Bearfence Mountain

SHENANDOAH

• Green Mountain 2149ft
Lewis Mountain
See detail map at right
⛺ 🎏 🛏 🚻 ♻ 3441ft
Lewis Mountain
Kirtley Mountain 2593ft
Naked Creek

3125ft The Oaks Overlook
• Piney Mountain 1975ft
Dry Run
60

Huckleberry Mountain 2158ft
ELKTON
Elk Run

South River Overlook 2950ft
South River 🚻 🎏 ♻
• Saddleback Mountain 3375ft

65
Swift Run Gap Entrance Station
2365ft 🏠
Hightop Mountain Parking 2637ft

211 340 / BUS 340

Campground

Big Meadows Campground
3655 U.S. Highway 211 East, Luray, VA 22835
(540) 999-3500
38.5286194, -78.438725

Day 54 *Activities.*

HIKE: Hazel Falls and Cave
5.1 mi 1005' elv 3:00 MODERATE

This gem of a cascade and pool is nestled amongst cliffs and a cave. Somehow this is an overlooked destination that you may have all to yourself.

The hike begins at the southern end of the Meadow Springs parking area by the cement post proclaiming "Hazel Mountain Rd.". The Buck Hollow Trail begins on the left but you will continue straight on the yellow-blazed Hazel Mountain Trail. The junction with the Buck Ridge Trail is reached at .4 miles, continue straight on the yellow-blazed trail. At 1.6 miles take a left at the junction on the yellow-blazed White Rocks Trail.

At 2.4 miles a cement post marks the junction with the blue-blazed Cave and Falls Trail. This is the steepest section of the hike with stone and man-made steps guiding you down the steepest section of the trail to the Hazel River. After the descent, where you reach the river, turn right and continue to follow the blue blaze trail. Hazel River Falls will appear on your left and the cave on your right. There is a nice pool just below this area as you approach the falls and cave.

Return the way you came in.

Location
38.6384300, -78.3136019

HIKE Brown's Gap Waterfall Loop
7.9 mi 1875' elv 4:30 MODERATE

What's not to love about a loop trail that follows creek beds most of the way.

From Brown's Gap, cross Skyline Drive and turn right, walk about 100 yards to the white-blazed Appalachian Trail. After a short steep incline, the AT levels out. Follow the AT heading south for 1.2 miles, passing the Dundo picnic area. At the Jones Run parking area, depart from the AT and turn left to join the blue-blazed Jones Run Trail descending into the valley below and cross over a stream that feeds into Jones Run. At 2.8 miles a cascade appears on the left. Jones Run Falls is slightly further down, just past a huge bolder. The trail now becomes the blue-blazed Doyles River Trail and the terrain becomes more uneven. The climb back up starts here.

Jones Run and later Doyles River flow beside the trail. Numerous small cascades, cataracts and stream crossings make this a beautiful section of the hike. At 4.2 miles reach Lower Doyles River Falls. Lower Doyles is the highest falls on this hike at 63'. Reach Upper Doyles River Falls at 4.5 miles, the smallest falls on the hike is only 28' but equally beautiful. Continue straight on the Doyle's River trail uphill for .9 miles and then take a left on the AT south 2 miles to Brown's Gap and the trailhead.

Location
38.2406365, -78.7108589

LOCATION	DISTANCE	TIME
🟢 Big Meadows Campground, VA	0 mi	0:00
🔵 Bushkill Falls, PA	324 mi	5:40
🔴 Albany, NY	474 mi	8:15
Total	474 mi	8:15

The Way Home

Savor this final day of your adventure.

Canada Goose

Day 55 *Activities*.

HIKE: Bushkill Falls
2mi 350' elv 1:30 EASY

Initially opened in 1904, this privately owned park is a popular tourist destination that features 8 waterfalls along a series of well developed trails.

THE FOUR TRAILS

Green Trail: This is the easiest and shortest trail at Bushkill Falls. It takes about 15 minutes to see the Main Falls.

Yellow Trail: The yellow trail is the most popular trail to take. It's relatively easy and will take approximately 45 minutes to complete. You'll see the Main Falls from several viewpoints, including the base of the falls.

Blue Trail: On the blue trail hikers will see Pennell Falls. It isn't that difficult and can be completed in about an hour and fifteen minutes.

Red Trail: The red trail is the longest of the four trails, at approximately 2 miles in length, and is the only trail with access to all eight waterfalls. It's also considered the most challenging trail.

Location
41.1174609, -75.0078025

"The Holy Land is everywhere."

- Black Elk

The End
Congratulations, you have completed the journey!

www.ingramcontent.com/pod-product-compliance
Lightning Source LLC
Chambersburg PA
CBHW040931030426
42334CB00007B/118